SELL MY HOME!

10 Steps to Finding a Buyer Today

Elna R. Tymes
Charles E. Prael

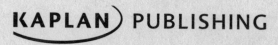

New York

This publication is designed to provide accurate and authoritative information in regard to the subject matter covered. It is sold with the understanding that the publisher is not engaged in rendering legal, accounting, or other professional service. If legal advice or other expert assistance is required, the services of a competent professional should be sought.

© 2008 by Elna Tymes and Charles E. Prael

Published by Kaplan Publishing, a division of Kaplan, Inc.
1 Liberty Plaza, 24th Floor
New York, NY 10006

Printed in the United States of America

May 2008
10 9 8 7 6 5 4 3 2 1

ISBN-13: 978-1-4277-9778-0

Kaplan Publishing books are available at special quantity discounts to use for sales promotions, employee premiums, or educational purposes. Please email our Special Sales Department to order or for more information at *kaplanpublishing@kaplan.com* or write to Kaplan Publishing, 1 Liberty Plaza, 24th Floor, New York, NY 10006.

Contents

Contents

Contents

Introduction

This book is a short, snappy guide to getting your house sold in today's difficult environment. The chapters are full of things you can do to improve the chances that you will find a buyer for your house in a relatively short time. It's based on real, time-tested strategies that lead to sales and focuses on things you can do to encourage the right buyers to come see your house—then buy it.

Aimed at the homeowner who needs to sell a house within three months or so, this book offers simple, easy-to-understand steps to researching the local market, finding the right REALTOR®, getting the house ready to show, staging the house, being prepared for financing options, using alternative marketing as well as the realtor's marketing tools, staging open houses, and using the negotiating process in a way that makes the buyer want to complete the sale.

According to the National Association of REALTORS®, approximately 5.5 million single-family homes in the United States were sold in 2007, down from a high of 7 million in 2005 and 6.5 million in 2006. Nationally, homes are taking longer to sell too: the current inventory of single-family homes is enough to fill current demand for another 10 months, and the inventory of condos and co-ops is enough for more than a year.

What This Book Will Do

This book doesn't contain any detailed speculation as to why homes aren't selling the way they used to, except to point out some basic characteristics of the market and the financing environment. Instead, the book focuses on how you can best deal with the current difficult environment of too many sellers and not enough buyers wanting to buy.

In these chapters, you'll learn about some cycles that determine whether you should sell now, how to analyze your local market, why your market may be different from one a few miles away, factors that help sell a house even in a down market, whether you should use a real estate agent, the importance of curb appeal, how to stage your house to enhance its appeal, how to use alterative marketing tactics, how to create financial options to attract more buyers, how to use exchanges and auctions, and how to negotiate a successful sale.

Location, Location, Location

Your local real estate market is different from others nearby, perhaps in big ways or perhaps only in small ways. Before you make changes to your house, and before your start to market your house, do some research in your local neighborhood as to what features appear in houses that sell.

Case in point. The flipping shows on television usually feature homes where the owners add granite countertops and stainless steel appliances to kitchens in addition to other upgrading touches. Frequently, these homeowners also upgrade bathrooms by trading molded tub and shower enclosures for lots of tile. Another common upgrade is the installation of all-wood floors.

While these touches are admirable and may be appreciated by most buyers, their cost has to be factored into the sale price of the house, and in some cases, they may make the house unaffordable to those who want to live in your neighborhood.

This book will help you look both for features that will help your house sell, in your neighborhood, and for tactics you can use to sell your house most effectively.

1

Why Do You Want to Sell?

Why are you selling your house right now?

Do you know about other options?

What are the trade-offs for selling right now versus waiting?

You're motivated! You've decided that you should sell your house now, and you need the best price you can get for it. You may be in a financial bind, or facing foreclosure, or having to move to another part of the country, or needing to sell because of a divorce or a death in the family. The bottom line is that you need to get your house on the market and you don't have a lot of time.

Before you put up the For Sale sign, take a few moments to consider your options.

Factors Beyond Your Control

You're going to have to accept some realities about the current market where you are. That means that you have to work with real estate cycles, seasonal buying preferences, lending cycles, and other factors such as the following:

- *Economic cycles.* Real estate goes through cycles of boom and bust. Sometimes these are related to national economic cycles, but sometimes they're local. A general economic recession usually means that financial institutions have less money to lend and that consumers are worried about their income streams.

- *Seasonal buying preferences.* Seasonal trends vary from place to place, but generally, buyers and sellers know that more houses will be available during the spring and summer, when moving is more convenient.

- *Lending cycles.* These also influence whether it's a good time to buy. Higher interest rates and tighter qualifying rules mean that fewer people will be able to afford a mortgage. On the other hand, lower rates and easier qualifying rules mean that more people will be looking.

Other factors that can influence whether it's a good time to sell your house include the state of the local economy, crime rates in your area, problems related to weather, and the general appearance of homes in your neighborhood.

If, for instance, your community has a single large employer who's announced a lot of layoffs, demand for houses in your area will probably be pretty low. If, however, unemployment is down and the local economy is growing, you stand a better chance of selling your house quickly.

If your house is in a high-crime area, buyers aren't as likely to be interested in your house. Ultimately, however, a low enough price can make your house interesting enough to attract a buyer.

Weather-related events, such as a flood or a landslide, can make your house undesirable, mostly because of buyer perception that the land on which your house sits is undesirable. Curiously, however, a direct hit by a tornado doesn't always devalue the neighborhood, since most homeowners rebuild fairly quickly, if they can.

Good local schools create their own demand. In an area with lots of choices, buyers—even those without children—gravitate toward areas with good schools, and the demand will tend to drive up prices, sometimes substantially.

Easy access to transportation corridors, particularly mass transit, can make a house more desirable than others located farther away. This is particularly true when the price of gasoline and other fuels is high.

Can You Afford to Wait?

Take a long look at why you think you need to sell right now. Are there things you can do to postpone your sale until a better time? Here are some examples:

■ If you're facing foreclosure, talk with your lender and see if listing your house for sale within the next 30 days will allow the lender to give you a postponement. Most financial institutions don't want to take your house, and if you're genuinely trying to sell it, they'll work with you.

■ If you're in another kind of financial bind and it's the wrong time of year to sell a house, see whether you can sell something else either to raise money or reduce your monthly payments. If you have an extra car, now might be the time to sell it. If you can borrow against your IRA or other pension plans or insurance policy, perhaps doing so will give you enough time to wait a few months. If you can afford it, using a margin plan will let you borrow against the value of your stock portfolio. And don't overlook the possibility of selling things you don't need through local want ads, online on Craig's List or eBay, or at a garage sale. Vintage clothing, for instance, sometimes brings surprisingly high prices. So does gold and some jewelry.

■ If you have to move to another part of the country and need to sell your house to buy another, consider renting a home in your new location while you wait for your house to sell. That approach will have the added benefit of giving you time to look around your new community and judge the best places to buy.

- If you need to sell because of a divorce or a death in the family, consider offering a lease with an option to buy to get the house occupied. You may not be able to get the money out of the house immediately, but it won't be vacant and neglected. If you're one of the parties in a divorce, see if you can work out a lease/option arrangement with your former partner while you wait for the market to get better.

In a Hurry?

Do you need to sell your house within the next 30 days? You don't have time to compensate for location or lending cycles or other factors. What are some things you can do right now to make a quick sale possible? Pay particular attention to Chapters 3, 4, 5, 6, and 7. You'll learn about pricing, hiring an agent, repairing house problems, cleaning up the clutter, creating good curb appeal, and staging.

Better Price Versus a Faster Sale

In most neighborhoods, a house with a lower price will sell faster than an equivalent house in the same neighborhood. If, however, the house with the lower price has been on the market for a long time, lowering the price may not bring in buyers faster. Buyers and even REALTORS® may get the impression that there's something wrong with the house other than the need to sell it. If you want to attract a quick sale, starting out with a price a bit lower than equivalent houses in the same neighborhood should provide the kind of interest you're after.

If you can't afford to lower your expected price, consider offering other incentives to make the overall price seem like a good value:

- Offer a quick close of escrow. If the buyer can have your house within 20 or 30 days, the deal may look better than a house where the buyer has to wait for 90 days.

- Offer to accept a small loan—usually a second mortgage—on your house as part of the sale. This will mean you won't get as much cash up front, but you're more likely to get your asking price.

- Offer an allowance toward newer or upgraded appliances if you're selling your house with the existing appliances. This tactic also will reduce the amount you'll get at close of escrow, but it may be just the incentive to get a quick sale.

- Offer some other benefit—such as a week in Hawaii—as an incentive for a quick close at your asking price. Depending on the time of year, you can find good hotel and plane fare packages on the Internet. In many cases, you'll pay less than $1,000 on airfare and a hotel for a week for two people.

Top 10 Checklist: Sell Your House Quicker

Every one of the things you're about to see may look simple. And, to be honest, a lot of them are—if you've been dealing with real estate for a while. But we've found that while a lot of people, even in the industry, know these things at a subconscious level, they can't explicitly state them. Which means, really, that they aren't thinking about them, nor are they intentionally applying them. And if they aren't intentionally applying them, then you've got a problem. Because that means you can't formulate a strategy around these basic precepts.

1. Realistic Pricing and Timing

The first thing you need to understand is that the days of pretty much automatically getting a better price than your neighbor are over. In many parts of the country, prices are going down, not up. Which means that pricing your house has become a lot more competitive now than two to three years ago.

In addition, you need to understand that underlying real estate cycles dictate the timing of when you are most likely to sell your house—and when you're going to have the most trouble.

Both of these factors mean that you're going to have to get very realistic about both the pricing and the timing of selling your house. What does being unrealistic get you? Well, it might mean that you sell your house for a pittance, or it might mean that you don't sell your house at all.

2. Who's Going to Sell Your House Successfully?

The next big item you need to address is, who is going to sell your house *successfully*. Not who's going to offer to sell it but who's actually going to put you across from a buyer. That person might be you, it might be your current real estate agent—or it might be someone new. But whoever it is, you need to know how to evaluate that person so that you find the right person to track, and bring back, the person who's going to buy your house.

3. Repairs and Upgrades

Quite a few people think that they need to repair or upgrade their house to get it to sell. Sometimes that's true. But you also need to understand the real cost/benefit analysis of doing that work—and go into it with your eyes wide open.

You should also understand that not all repairs or upgrades are done to get a better price. Instead, they may be done to help your house sell faster—to get more people in the door and improve your ability to market your home against the others in your neighborhood.

4. Clean Up and Clean Out

The simple reality is, most people don't like to buy cluttered houses. If you've got lots of stuff all over the place, it is a guaranteed distraction for potential buyers.

Therefore, to improve your ability to sell your house, quickly, you need to reduce that clutter. Clean up and clean out!

5. First Impressions Count: Curb Appeal

One of the basic rules of real estate is that you can't get someone to like the inside of your house if they aren't willing to come in the front door. That's where curb appeal comes in—making your house inviting from the moment when someone pulls up.

6. Staging

Cleaning out a house is one thing, especially if you've already moved. But how do you really make your house look its very best when the time comes to show it? That's where staging comes in. From the mundane to the fancy, there are a large number of ways to improve the look of your house. Some of these choices can be as simple as reorganizing what you already have.

7. Alternative Marketing

So your real estate agent has put your house on the multiple-listing service (MLS) and held open houses, and you just aren't getting anyone to bite. In the world of real estate, there are many other ways to get out the word about your house, including a number of options that have popped up only in the last few years.

8. Creative Financing

One especially troublesome area in the current market is when potential buyers seek bank financing. That being said, a number of creative solutions to financing your home can make that process easier—or even make it possible where it previously wasn't.

9. Exchanges

Over the past few years, 1031 exchanges have become a very popular way to "sell" a property and "buy" another, without incurring the potentially huge tax liability involved in a sale. Besides potentially favorable tax treatment, 1031 exchanges have other benefits, such as allowing you to make a transaction happen quickly and giving you more flexibility in making a transaction happen.

10. Auctions

Most people don't pay attention to the fact that almost *any* house will sell, given the right price. Auctions are one way to find that "right price" in almost any market. Bear in mind, though, that there are both pros and cons to auctioning off your property.

3

Step 1: Realistic Pricing and Timing

Do you know what your house is worth in today's market?

Is it the wrong time to sell?

Learn how to price your house for the market that currently exists, regardless of market conditions or real estate or lending cycles.

All real estate is *local.* What that means is that when buying or selling a house, the most important factors influencing a sale are local ones, such as the presence or lack of a nearby urban area, the reputation of local schools, shopping and transportation amenities, and the quality of the neighborhood.

The most important thing you can do when trying to sell your house is to know the truth about the local market conditions. That means knowing what's currently selling and knowing when it's a good time (or a bad time) to be selling.

What's Your House Really Worth?

You may have an inflated idea of what your house is worth based on old information or mistaken ideas about how much certain features are valued. Or you may have underestimated the value of your house. In any case, it's very important that you get some objective data that helps you correctly set your expectations.

Real estate values, particularly house prices, are usually based on recent sale prices of comparable properties nearby.

Recent usually means within the last six months. Market conditions can vary widely over the course of a year due to economic conditions, a changing lending market, the number of homes on the market, or other local factors, so what was true a year ago may not be true now. Rising unemployment in your area, for instance, may reduce the number of potential buyers and result in more homes staying on the market longer than, say, a year ago. Sellers may be forced to accept a lower price than the original listing price just to get the house sold.

Sale prices are more important than asking prices. Asking prices are what the seller thinks the house can get. Sales prices are what reasonable buyers are willing to pay. An unrealistically high asking price may cause a house to stay on the market a long time. If you want your house to sell, set your asking price close to the average sale price of similar houses nearby.

Houses *comparable* to yours have not only the same number of bedrooms and bathrooms but are roughly the same size, sit on lots that are about the same size, and have the same kinds of amenities. If you have an in-ground swimming pool or spa and nearby comparable houses don't, you may have a feature that makes your house worth more (or in some areas, less). A landscaped backyard is usually worth more than an unlandscaped backyard. A house on a busy street is usually worth less than a house on a quiet street.

Local usually means in the same neighborhood or area, rarely more than five miles away. In an urban area, *local* means within a mile. A house five miles away may be in a better school district, have a spectacular view, or be in a gated community or in a high crime area and, hence, is not really comparable to yours.

Where do you find comparable local, recent prices? By law, sale prices of real estate are recorded in your local tax assessor's office. (This is so that the assessor can send out accurate tax bills.) When you receive your tax bill, you usually also receive a statement regarding your house's "assessed value." Many county assessors' offices also have online Web pages, where you can check for this figure for your house. That will give you a starting point. But assessed value and market value are two different things, sometimes very different, and you're after *market value*.

Another way to check the market value of your house is to look online at some of the public Web sites. One of those is Zillow (*www.zillow.com*), a free site that lets you see the value of your house and that of houses nearby. When you enter your address, the map displays a satellite view of your house and the surrounding neighborhood, with yellow flags showing houses that recently sold, along with their prices, number of bedrooms and bathrooms, and size, and red flags indicating houses for sale. Houses without flags haven't sold recently but have data including a computed market value and other information. Because of the formulas it uses, Zillow's market values may be higher or lower than the market values a local real estate agent may report.

You can also use the value calculators that are frequently a free feature on the Web pages of local real estate agents, lending institutions, and some insurance companies.

Your local real estate agent is usually willing to give you an "estimate of market value" based on the agent's knowledge of the area. This represents a summary of what this agent knows about properties in your local area that have sold recently. The problem with this type of report is that some agents do a good job of research and some don't.

A more rigorous type of analysis is called an "appraisal," and a fee is usually charged for it. Appraisals are done by real estate agents who have specific credentials for this kind of work. Appraisers are usually hired by lending institutions to determine the actual market value of your property, and the amount of money you can borrow against your house is based on its appraised value.

Why Appraisals Don't Necessarily Matter

Any appraisal or estimate of market value for your house will rely on recent sales in your area. Many times, however, other factors influence the marketability of your house, and these can add or subtract hundreds or even thousands of dollars.

Appraisals are usually paid for by the seller, because the seller benefits from knowing the value of the house. Appraisals are required when you apply for a mortgage, because the lender needs to know that there is enough equity to protect the financial institution's interest (the loan amount). Appraisals are a good thing to have when trying to set a price for your house, because the research that backs up an appraisal is fairly objective.

That said, however, appraisers are human beings and some-times make mistakes. We've seen a number of appraisers recently who ask what the homeowner wants to see as a market value and then try to pick data that support that number, regardless of actual sale prices of comparable houses. We've also seen appraisers who don't understand the value of some factors. For instance, only recently have we seen appraisers who add value for solar roof panels and a solar heating system.

Further, there's a big difference between a formal appraisal done by a certified appraiser and an estimate of market value done by a local REALTOR®. The former has to meet quantitative and qualitative standards for appraisal, and the appraisal process involves measuring the house (and sometimes the rooms) to determine actual square footage, uses only sales data that can be independently verified, and is done by carefully comparing features in similar local houses. The latter doesn't have to abide by the same strict rules.

What Makes Homes Sell Locally

The following is a list of some factors that we've found to make a house sell fast:

- A price that's slightly lower than the median price for comparable local houses in good condition

- Flexible financing. The seller understands that a tight mortgage market means that buyers may need a bit of help in order to put together the transaction.

- A house that's bright, clean and neat, with no clutter

- A house with no deferred maintenance—in move-in condition

- A house with a recently upgraded kitchen and bathrooms

- Landscaping that looks fresh and well tended

- A clearly usable backyard, devoid of junk and overgrown plants

- A finished patio area for outdoor entertaining

- A warm, inviting feeling when one first steps through the front door

- A real estate agent who promptly answers all questions, is prepared with handouts, and works to get a transaction through escrow as quickly as possible

Good Times and Bad Times to Sell a House

Real estate goes through cycles of boom and bust. Sometimes these are related to national economic cycles, but sometimes they're local. A general economic recession usually means that there's less money to lend and that consumers are worried about their income stream. If people aren't sure that their jobs are going to be around in six months, they aren't likely to consider a big purchase, like a home. When a lot of people are hesitant, then regardless of how nice your home appears, it may not fetch many buyers unless you price it below others in your current local market. You may even have to take a loss.

Seasonal buying preferences are another factor. Other factors being equal, buying interest picks up about the middle of January in some places or after the snowstorms stop in others. Buyer interest continues to rise through June or July, then begins to drop off. Most places experience a low period in sales from the middle of November through the middle of January. This will vary from place to place, but generally buyers and sellers know that more houses will be available during the spring and summer, when moving is more convenient.

Lending cycles also influence whether it's a good time to buy. Higher interest rates and tighter qualifying rules mean that fewer people can afford a mortgage. Lower rates and easier qualifying rules mean that more people are looking. If you need to sell in a lending cycle where interest rates are high or qualifying rules are tight, you may have to do a little creative financing to sell your house. See Chapter 10 for some suggestions.

Why Days-on-Market Matters

The longer a house has been on the market, even with adjustments in price, the less likely it is to sell.

Why is this?

Once a house has been on the market for a month or so, most real estate agents assume that anyone who is in the market for a new house has already seen this house and either expressed interest or dismissed it. Some factors, such as having the house come on the market in December or at the beginning of a period of bad weather, can deter those who are looking.

If your house has been on the market for more than 60 days and no one's made an offer, you can assume that peak interest has passed and it's time to try something else.

Warning: If your house has been unoccupied for more than 30 days, it may get "discovered" by thieves who make off with furniture, appliances, cupboards, copper piping, and anything else that can be sold.

Why Homes Don't Sell

Buyers naturally want to maximize the value they get for their dollars. We've seen the following mistakes made by homeowners:

- An unrealistically high price

  Solution: Either reduce the price or add some incentives, such as the ones we discussed in Chapter 1 and those in Chapter 10.

- Putting a For Sale sign in the yard but doing nothing else to publicize or market the house

  Solution: Publicize the sale through multiple-listing services, holding open houses, and listing the house in the local want ads. Create a Web page "tour" of your house with a video camera and put the address of the page (its URL) on your For Sale sign.

- Listing with a no-frills REALTOR® who doesn't market the house or hold open houses.

  Solution: Either market the house yourself and hold well-publicized open houses or switch to a full-service REALTOR®.

- Failure to clean up the front yard

  Solution: Clean it up. NOW.

- Too many cars, particularly old cars, in the driveway

  Solution: Get rid of the cars. Either give them to charity (you can usually get a tax deduction) or get them hauled to a local junkyard. If your household regularly uses the cars, park anything over two cars on the street or somewhere else.

- Structural, plumbing, electrical, or heating problems that are too expensive for the buyer to fix

  Solution: If you can't fix the problem yourself, get an estimate of what it would cost to fix the problem and give the buyer a rebate for that amount in escrow. If you can't afford to pay for it all, consider a barter arrangement with the contractor.

- Failure to clean up the inside of the house. This is a big one and can include everything from cleaning up the clutter to cleaning the bathrooms.

  Solution: If you can't or won't clean up the house, hire a cleaning service to do it for you. Then maintain the house in that condition.

These are all things that the homeowner can easily change and that might make the difference between the home's selling and just sitting on the market.

Other possible reasons why a house may not sell have nothing to do with the way it looks:

- Location, location, location. If the house is in a flood plain, in a high-crime area, or next to an undesirable area—such as a junkyard—buyers will probably look elsewhere.

    Solution: Offer buyers an incentive to reconsider your house. If your house is in a flood plain, consider paying for flood insurance. If you're in a high-crime area, consider paying for a year's worth of security services. If the nearby junkyard attracts rodents, consider adding two years of pest service as an incentive.

- Owners who either can't or won't negotiate terms of a sale, particularly regarding existing loans

    Solution: Allowing a buyer to take over existing loans can sometimes make the difference between a sale and no sale.

- Title problems that prevent the new owner from getting a clean title to the property at close of escrow

    Solution: Either clean up the title yourself or offer an incentive to the buyer to assume the title under existing conditions.

- If a house has been empty and for sale for too long, it may have been discovered by transients and other squatters, who may have trashed the inside.

    Solution: Prevent the problem by either living in the house yourself or offering it as a short-term rental so that at least it's occupied. Make sure the tenants keep up the property and are cooperative with realtors. If the damage has already occurred, either make the necessary repairs and clean up the property, or reduce the price by an amount that will cover repairs. Some people are willing to take on the challenges posed by a property in disrepair, but are likely to make a low offer. Be willing to negotiate.

Step 2: Who Will Successfully Sell Your House?

Note: In this book, we use the terms "Realtor®" and "realtor." A Realtor® is a member of the National Association of Realtors, a professional association for those in the real estate industry. A realtor, in this book, refers to anyone who is licensed in your state to act as a real estate agent, although not necessarily a member of the *National Association of Realtors*.

We're assuming that you've already been trying to sell your house and it hasn't sold. You've just run into the problem that many sellers face—who's actually going to *sell* the house?

The funny thing is, finding a realtor isn't necessarily that hard. We're sure you know one. Maybe you know more—in some parts of the country, it seems as though you can't swing a cat without hitting another realtor.

The real issue, therefore, isn't "how do I find a realtor?" Rather, it's "how do I find a realtor who can sell my house in a timely manner?" The problem is that while your cousin Vinnie might be a realtor to whom you want to give the deal, if he can't make a sale happen, perhaps it's time to find someone who will have more success.

How much of a difference can this make? Well, let us use one neighborhood that we happen to be familiar with as an example. Since this summer, about a dozen homes in this neighborhood have come on the market with, basically, four different results:

1. One house was listed via a realtor who's apparently fairly new to the neighborhood. It's been on the market for three months, and hasn't budged.

2. One house was listed via a limited-service realtor. It's been pulled from the market, but hasn't sold.

3. One house was listed as For Sale By Owner (a FSBO). It's been on the market for five months and hasn't moved.

4. Ten other houses were listed via experienced, effective realtors—people who *sell*. Every one of those homes sold within 30 days, for more than the asking price, including one that was priced over $100,000 above the norm for the neighborhood. Oh, and three realtors did all that.

Ask Your Friends and Neighbors

One really straightforward way to find a realtor who's effective at selling is to ask your friends and neighbors if they know any good realtors. The people you really want to ask are the ones who've bought or sold a house within the last

18 months. They have personal experience dealing with a realtor who has effectively sold a property, either on their behalf or to them. They can tell you who was effective—and who wasn't.

Finding Realtors Who Have Been Selling Recently

Another way to find a realtor who is making sales happen is to have someone check on the multiple-listing service (MLS) for transactions that have closed in your neighborhood in the last six months. Generally, this requires going through an intermediary, but you might try calling the receptionists at some of the local brokerages and asking if they can help you find a "good" realtor. Tell them you're looking for someone who's sold houses in your neighborhood recently and that you're really interested in their days-on-market numbers. Remember those, from Chapter 3? Here's where you get to apply that statistic. Lower days-on-market numbers mean faster sales.

Realtors Who Sell Versus Realtors Who Just List

One problem, especially in large metropolitan areas, is that a lot of people have real estate agent licenses. (For example, in the San Francisco Bay Area, there are over 14,000 licensed real estate agents, or about 1 agent per 512 people). But the vast majority of those agents really don't have either the experience or the talent that you need. And when it comes to selling real estate in challenging circumstances, you want both experience *and* talent on your side.

Part of the problem is that quite a few realtors think that doing all the "normal" things—listing a property on the MLS, holding open houses, and so forth—is still all that's required to sell a house. A few years ago, in a seller's market, that might have been enough. But that's just not the case any more.

Commission Rates: Pro and Con

*"Satisfy what's in your left hand
before reaching with your right." — Dave's Rules*

One common trap that we've seen homesellers get into is obsessing over how much they can knock down the commission rate. This is a trap because it really doesn't matter if you get a lower rate if selling the house takes significantly longer or it doesn't sell at all. Saving $5,000–$10,000 in commission fees isn't necessarily a bad thing—if it works out.

The thing you need to bear in mind, though, is that the commission savings are only a potential savings—they only apply once your house has sold. But the expenses you incur in the meantime are real, with cash coming out of your pocket. Because, as we already know, your house hasn't sold yet, you need to make a bit of a judgment call.

Sometimes, however, the judgment call just comes down to straight economics. Is saving one point in commission, worth maybe $6,000, worth paying a couple extra months of house payments, say at $3,000 a month? In that case, going with the "cheaper" solution just doesn't make a lot of sense. It would actually cost you money.

One good way to sort this out is to pencil out the numbers involved. Doing so is pretty straightforward. All you need to do is make a conservative estimate of how long it will take for your house to sell and do two columns of addition.

In the left column, put down the following numbers:

- The total commission cost you'll pay with your discount realtor
- Your expenses for the number of months you think it will take to sell your house

In the right column, put down the following numbers:

- The total commission cost you'll pay with a selling-oriented realtor
- Your expenses for the number of months your selling-oriented realtor will need to sell your house

Now add up the two columns and see which one comes out smaller. You might be surprised.

Checking References

Before finalizing your choice of a new real estate agent, make sure that you get, and check, references.

This is important because you need to find out, from someone with experience with your potential realtor, what that agent's actual sales performance is like.

What questions should you ask when you check references? We find that the following questions cover the important issues:

- How long did it take the agent to sell your house? Do you have any idea of the average time in your neighborhood for a property to sell?

- Without getting into specifics, were you pleased with the price that you received for your sale?

- Did you run into any issues while working with your agent?

Also, before finalizing a selection, you should ask your potential agent for a marketing proposal for your house.

Should You Try a FSBO?

Every prospective homeseller thinks about doing a FSBO. After all, if you do a FSBO, you can keep at least half of the commission money (maybe all, if you and your buyer hook up directly). Plus there's the "I can do *that!*" aspect.

However, speaking as people who have bought and sold a number of properties over the years, we view FSBOs in the same way that judges view people who choose to represent themselves in court: ("A man who represents himself has a fool for a client and a fool for a lawyer.") Why? Because of four issues:

1. *Training.* One thing that every real estate agent will bring to the table without fail is a certain minimum level of training in the legalities required to sell a house. And don't kid yourself: any "standard" sale requires you to do a certain amount of legally required paperwork, without exception, especially if some form of financing is involved. Agents are trained in dealing with that stuff.

2. *Resources.* Because they're part of a larger organization, agents usually have access to better resources than you would. Almost any realtor will have access to the local Multiple Listing Service (MLS), for example—something you, as an individual owner, won't be able to touch. They'll be able to schedule your house into their brokerage's agent tours. And they'll have access to the in-house legal and financial backup that helps make a transaction happen.

3. *Use of your time.* This is one item that most people don't think about. Basically, it comes down to a question of what's a more efficient and effective use of time—really an economic issue. If your time is valueless, maybe spending all of it marketing your home *is* a good use of your time. But if you're working, then trying to market your home on top of your day job could be unfeasible. And not having time to market your house properly could be a real killer when it comes to reaching potential buyers.

4. *Marketing reach.* Because they have more time and access to better resources, real estate agents tend to be able to market to more people, more effectively, than you.

All that said, FSBOs do work, on occasion. However, they're certainly not for the faint of heart or those of you who are busy during the day.

Using Limited-Service Realtors

Something new that's cropped up in the last few years is the limited-service real estate agency. These agencies provide the basic services you might expect from a realtor—but that's about it. In return, rather than taking a percentage of the value of the house as their fee, they take a smaller fixed fee. In return you, the owner, wind up shouldering a portion of the workload.

We've never been a fan of limited-service realtors. In many ways, they combine the worst aspects of both listing agents and FSBOs. They don't provide any particularly effective marketing services other than the basics. They don't do any of the other work that you might reasonably expect from an agent, which is actually very critical to selling your house, though they do help you through the closing. And they leave you, the owner, to deal with much of the on-the-ground work of marketing and showing your home, which takes a lot of time and energy.

There's one more thing to realize about both limited-service realtors and FSBOs. They are both strategies that are optimal for a seller's market. In today's buyer's market, however, these strategies do not perform well.

5

Step 3: Repairs and Upgrades

One question that most homesellers approach with trepidation is the whole subject of repairs and upgrades. Most people think of this as just a cost issue—can you afford to spend the money? In reality, it touches on other aspects of selling your house, including whether someone will make an offer and whether they'll be more interested in buying your house versus another in the same neighborhood.

Analysis

Before you start thinking about repairing or upgrading your house, take a look at other, similar houses in your neighborhood that are on the market. Because the current market is a buyer's market, you and those other homeowners are competing for a relatively small set of buyers. Knowing your competition is simply a matter of doing your homework.

Similar Houses in Your Neighborhood

First, you want to tour the other houses in your neighborhood that are on the market. You want to concentrate on houses that are similar to yours in terms of overall characteristics: size, number of bedrooms/bathrooms, price range, and so forth. Weekend open houses are often good opportunities for looking.

When you go, bring a notepad and take notes of how these other houses might show better than yours. If you see a particular approach that you like—how they handled window dressings, for example—take notes on what they did and how they did it.

That said, you probably don't want to advertise blatantly to the realtors hosting these open houses that you're shopping the competition. Be a bit noncommittal: tell them that you're interested in houses in the area and thought you'd look around a bit.

Analyze Your Own House

Once you've looked at the other houses in your neighborhood, take a look at your house, analyzing it the same way. One of the most important things you can do is to step back from the viewpoint of "this is my home" and look at it from the perspective of a potential buyer. Use the same viewpoint on your house as when looking at those other houses. Note everything that you now thinks needs fixing to make the house more marketable.

When you're done, you've got the beginnings of a list of things you can do to fix your house up to make it sell.

Making Repairs

Repairs are one of those problematic decisions. They are, ultimately, a maintenance cost for which *somebody* has to pay. The question is, will that person be you or your buyer?

When you look at repairs, you should categorize every item into one of three areas:

1. Things that need to be addressed to make the house sell
2. Things that need to be addressed but can be paid for out of escrow
3. Things that you'd like to address but don't need to be addressed

Within those categories, you should prioritize items by what's going to help the most. If you are already working with a realtor, talk it over with your agent, who will generally know what makes the most sense for your area.

We can't give you hard and fast rules to follow, but here are a few guidelines that are helpful:

■ If something is in reasonably decent repair and is fully functional, it can either be put off entirely or paid for out of escrow. If, for example, your roof is in decent shape—not new but also not with the shingles falling apart—then you may be able to ignore it or push it off until escrow, depending on what a buyer might want.

■ If something is obviously not functional, you should probably try to address it. To use the previous example, if your roof is obviously leaking, you should at least repair the leaking spots and repaint the ceiling. Having visible water spots on your ceiling is a sure way to get potential buyers wondering what problems they *can't* see.

■ Some repairs are worth extra money. Again using the roof as an example, putting a new roof on to deal with an old, tired one is a good way to increase the value of your house to a potential buyer.

All that being said, you'd be amazed what a fresh coat of paint can do to a room. Just remember to be neat and tidy while you're painting—use drop cloths, masking tape, and so forth and try for a professional look.

To Upgrade or Not?

A recent article on Yahoo! News made the interesting assertion that upgrades to a house aren't an investment but rather an expense—a livability expense but an expense nonetheless. To some extent, the statement is true. But if you're trying to sell your house, that expense can also be looked at as a marketing cost, one of many things you can do to make your house more interesting and salable than another.

Why, you ask? Because if you have upgraded the house, even partially, you've made it more inviting for the new buyer.

Pimp That House!

Upgrades attract buyers like moths to a candle. At a given price, for two equally-sized houses, buyers will go for the upgraded one 9 times out of 10. Allow us to illustrate.

About a year ago, we wound up dealing with a run-down tract house in California. The front was nicely kept, and the previous owners had started (but not finished) a remodel of the master bathroom. But that was it. The backyard was a mess, and the rest of the house looked much the way it had when it was built—in 1965. So what did we do?

- We finished the bathroom remodel (the main expense was retiling the shower).

- We rebuilt the kitchen, using prefab cabinets and laminate countertop from a home store. We put in the *cheapest* dishwasher we could find, still an upgrade because there hadn't been one previously. And we reused the old stove in our new kitchen by the simple expedient of cleaning it to within an inch of its life.

- We cleaned up the back yard and fixed the (falling down) fence.

■ We made a few other changes here and there, like cleaning up the partially completed closet reconstruction and tidying up the cable and phone wiring.

What happened? Well, that house, in a nondescript neighborhood, with four other similar houses on the market, sold within two weeks for a price a bit above what we'd been expecting. Admittedly, that's an extreme example, but it illustrates a point: We'd made our house nicer than the competition, and it paid off.

Getting the Best Bang for Your Buck

So the next question is, where to put your dollar to work in your house. Remember that list you made of all the things you liked about the other houses on the market? Now is the time to use it. Everything that follows, you can do. The primary considerations you need to keep in mind are

■ Safety first

■ Careful and professional-looking will always win out over rushed and haphazard

■ A little elbow grease and the right materials can go a long way.

So let's look at some simple, high-return changes you can make to your house.

Kitchen

There are a number of inexpensive ways to upgrade your kitchen:

- *Refinish your cabinets.* Depending on the cabinets you have, repainting them or placing new doors on old cabinets can enhance the look of your kitchen without spending a lot of money. Doors can be had from most home stores—just make sure you have accurate dimensions from your existing doors before you run off to buy new ones. Paint, of course, is cheaper. On a related note, if your kitchen is small or dark, consider using a lighter finish to help brighten up the room.

- *Knobs and pulls.* Another way to upgrade the look of a kitchen cheaply is to replace the knobs and pulls with modern ones. Again, these can be had from hardware stores and often just require a screwdriver to replace.

- *Countertops.* Depending on the condition of your counters, you might consider putting in new ones. A lot here depends on what you have, what you can do, and what you think is reasonable. But decent laminate countertops for an entire kitchen can be had for under $200, and properly installed, they can easily spruce up the room's look. If you're really feeling ambitious, we've been seeing low-end granite sheet countertops ready to install for $70–$80 per 8-foot slab. Of course, that doesn't include the cost of backsplashes, sink or appliance cut-outs, or any other work that might be required. Another alternative might be granite tiles, which are less expensive than granite slabs.

■ *Updating the faucet.* With today's pricing, a new, multifunction kitchen faucet can be had for $40–$50, and it makes the kitchen that much more attractive. If you have never done this kind of thing before, make sure to talk with the folks at the store about how to do the installation before you leave. And remember to tag the hot and cold water lines so you don't mix them up!

Bathrooms

Most of what was said about kitchens also applies to bathrooms, especially refinishing the cabinets, replacing knobs and pulls (and other hardware, like towel rods, if they look really worn), and updating the faucet and shower/bath hardware. Bringing a coherent look to a bathroom by installing matching fixtures also helps.

Paint

Paint is a great way to make many problems disappear. Fresh paint, properly applied, can both freshen and brighten your house, and if you're doing it yourself all you pay for is the materials and a few tools.

■ *Use decent tools.* We've found that the really cheap rollers and brushes (the five for $10 specials, for example) tend to produce spotty results, which you either have to redo or just plain look bad. Investing a few extra dollars in decent brushes and rollers will pay off later in easier painting and a better-looking job.

■ *Use neutral colors.* Strong colors are great for strong reactions—but that might mean someone really *doesn't* like your paint job.

■ *Patch every hole, dent, and crack* that you can before you paint. Part of the point of the exercise is to make your walls look new and clean. Holes, cracks, dents all detract from that look.

■ *Apply multiple coats* to get a really smooth finish. First, prime the wall. Sand the primer with 220-grit sandpaper once it's dried, then wipe it down with a damp cloth. Apply the first coat of latex paint, then sand and wipe that coat. Finally apply your top coat of latex.

■ *Semigloss paints* will make your walls seem brighter.

■ *Flat paints* are better for hiding dents or cracks but show dirt easily, and they're harder to clean.

Electrical Fixes

■ *Update outlets with Ground Fault Interruption (GFI) protection.* Most older kitchens and bathrooms use standard outlets. Modern electrical codes, however, insist on GFI breakers. For about $11–$12 per outlet, you can update your kitchen or bathroom to include GFI breakers. Just remember that the only outlets that need to be updated are those supplying power to the rest of the outlets on a circuit. In a bathroom, that may mean that you only need a single GFI outlet.

■ *Update switches and outlets.* Many new-style outlets and switches can be installed using the existing electrical cabling in your house. Using newer outlets and switches gives the impression that the electrical wiring is also new. Using dimmer switches in selected locations, like the living room and bedrooms, can help as well. If you change the outlet or switch, though, remember to get a matching new plate for it as well. Using old plates with new outlets or switches is a guaranteed giveaway of what you've done.

■ *Change out selected light fixtures.* If you're feeling up to it, you might consider updating some of your light fixtures. Cheap, nice fixtures can be had for under $40 at your local hardware/home store—for considerably less if you get less fancy. While you're at it, you might consider switching to fluorescent from incandescent bulbs, which are more energy efficient and often cheaper.

■ Depending on your local climate, ceiling fans can be a great upgrade to a built-in light, and they can often be had from big-box stores for only $20–$30.

A note on changing outlets and switches: *Before* you do any electrical work, make sure you identify the circuit that you're working on and turn off power to either that circuit or the whole house. Changing out switches and outlets on a hot, live circuit is dangerous, even deadly.

6

Step 4: Clean Up and Clean Out

You may not be able to sell your house unless it's clean, inside and out. And that includes removing all the clutter. A clean house is inviting. It easily lets people picture themselves and their possessions in that setting, giving them a blank slate in which to design their own use of the space.

Chances are your house isn't as sparkling clean as it should be when put on the market. This chapter gives you some check-lists of things you can do, room by room, to get your house in condition for sale.

Cleaning Up

You may find that getting your house cleaned up for sale is a daunting process. If you approach it room by room, however, it may not be so overwhelming.

Kitchen

In most cases, the kitchen is the room that matters the most. You don't have to get it squeaky clean, but attention to details will help it make a good impression.

- Start with the cupboards. You may not make it to the upper levels, but empty out the first level of the upper cupboards and clean the shelf, preferably with a household cleaner that contains ammonia. The ammonia smell will linger and give a fleeting impression of sanitary conditions. Then line the lower shelf with new shelf paper, or butcher paper. When you put things back, try to make them orderly and neat so that they'll make a good impression when a prospective buyer opens the cupboard.

- At least straighten out the contents of the other shelves as well. An orderly cupboard suggests cleanliness.

- Repeat the process with the cupboards under the counter. Line the lower shelves with fresh shelf paper.

- Clean the countertops with a household cleaner, being sure to remove stains and watermarks. Move most of the countertop items to other locations so that the countertops look uncluttered.

- Thoroughly wash and polish the floors. Be sure to sweep up all the crumbs that collect in the kick space under the cupboards. Pull out the refrigerator and sweep up the dust that collects under and behind it.

- If you have a kitchen table or eating area, be sure the surface is clean. You may want to set the table with place mats, cutlery, and plates to make it inviting. Or set out a small bowl of fresh flowers or fresh fruit.

■ Clean the cupboard doors with a good wood cleaner. You'd be surprised how much kitchen grease and dust accumulates on cupboard doors over the years. If you can afford to do so, replace the door handles with new hardware. While you're at it, replace the drawer pulls too.

■ Clean the oven and cooktop. If you have a self-cleaning oven, run the cleaning cycle and then clean up the accumulated ash. If the cooktop is not a sealed design, remove the burner grates and clean out the area under the heat source. Replace burner liners with clean aluminum liners.

■ Clean the top of the refrigerator. Some people like to run a finger across the top of the refrigerator to judge whether a kitchen is clean enough, and you don't want them turned off by a finger full of dust.

■ If you have a tile countertop, clean the grout with a small brush or old toothbrush. Also, clean the edges where the sink meets the countertop.

■ Use a cloth around a broom or a vacuum cleaner to remove spiderwebs from the ceiling.

■ If you have a kitchen window with curtains, wash and iron the curtains and clean the window.

■ Before you show your house, clean the kitchen sink and get rid of any spots or scrapes. A sparkling sink implies that the rest of the kitchen is also clean.

Bathrooms

The room that has the next-highest impact is the master bathroom. This needs to be even more spotless than the kitchen. And it must smell clean. Try these tips:

- Wash the bathroom floor carefully, including behind the toilet, around the joint where the toilet meets the floor, and where the bathtub or shower meets the floor.

- Carefully clean the tub, the shower, the bathroom sink, and the toilet. You want no spots or discolorations. Use a special cleaner to remove any standing rings in the toilet. Use a small swab to clean dirty corners or edges in the tub or around the shower door.

- Clean any windows, mirrors, and lights.

- Inspect the walls for spots and fingerprints. Be sure to clean any switch plates, door jambs, door edges, and areas around door handles.

- Use a cloth around a broom to remove spiderwebs from the ceiling.

- If you have tile, clean the grout with a small brush or a used toothbrush.

- Be sure to clean the toothbrush holder and the area around it.

Living Room, Dining Room, and Family Room

Most prospective buyers come through the front door into the living room, so they get their first impression of a house's interior from that room. Luckily, cleaning a living room, dining room, or family room is usually easier than cleaning a kitchen or bathroom.

- Vacuum or clean the floor thoroughly. If you have area rugs, roll them out of the way and clean underneath them. Move furniture so that you can clean under couches, tables, and chairs.

- If you have a fireplace, shovel out the ashes and sweep the hearth. Arrange wood so that it looks ready for a fire.

- Dust everything, especially the TV screen.

- Neatly arrange any magazines, books, or knickknacks you want to display. Put yesterday's newspaper in the recycling area.

- If you have indoor plants, clip off and discard any dead leaves or spent blooms. Make sure they look as if they're well cared for.

- Clear off and dust the dining room table, then arrange a pretty tablecloth and centerpiece or set the table.

- Clean all the windows, inside and out.

- Use a vacuum cleaner to remove dust from any drapes or curtains and arrange them to show off the windows. Remove any torn window coverings.

Bedrooms

Each bedroom should look inviting and relaxing, even if it's a child's room. The master bedroom in particular should look clean and uncluttered.

- Make the beds, every day. Bed linens don't have to be new, but they do need to look clean.

- Straighten things in closets. Prospective buyers will open closet doors to get a sense of how big the closets are and will be put off by things spilling out onto the floor.

- Vacuum and dust thoroughly, including removing cobwebs.

- Clean any smudges around door jambs, door edges, door handles, and switch plates.

- Clean the windows and curtains.

Garage

Many people don't store cars in their garages—they store things that won't fit elsewhere. Especially if your garage is full of miscellaneous stuff, cleaning it up can help sell your house.

- Can you get rid of some of the stuff in your garage? Maybe you can hold a garage sale. Or maybe you can rent a small storage unit for a couple of months. Aim for where you could store a car in the garage if you wanted to.

- Buy some industrial metal shelves and arrange things you need to keep on the shelves.

- Inspect your garage for evidence of termites or other pests, and have pest control people remove the problem. Be sure you get a receipt to show prospective buyers about the inspection and remediation.

- Arrange tools by functional groups, preferably off the floor.

- Consider laying a sheet of plywood across the rafters and storing some items above the rafters.

- Sweep the garage floor thoroughly. Remove any spiderwebs on the walls.

- Clean any garage windows.

Outside

A prospective buyer's first impression comes from the front entrance to your house. Stand across the street and look at your house as if you were a potential buyer.

- Do shrubs and trees hide the face of your house? Consider trimming them back to make your house more visible.

- Is there a clear path to your front door? If there's a walkway, make sure no debris is in the way, that edges are clearly defined, and that there's adequate lighting.

- Rake and dispose of any dead leaves. Mow the lawn if necessary. If your lawn needs watering to make it green, do so. If it's seasonally brown, just make sure it's neat.

- Remove any dead annuals from planting beds.

- The side and backyards count too. However, rather than considering them an entrance to your house, look at them as places for outdoor entertaining or functional additions, such as a vegetable garden.

- Get rid of any junk. A prospective buyer doesn't want to look at it either.

- Clean up the barbecue and area around it. If you have chairs and a table for outdoor entertaining, arrange them in an inviting way, unless they've been put away for the winter.

- Sweep any decks or concrete areas.

Cleaning Out

Many homeowners have a difficult time understanding that there's a difference between presenting your house the way you live in it and presenting your house for sale. With the former, your personal tastes matter—in color choices, in furniture, in familiar things, even with the degree of clutter. With the latter, you're trying to appeal to people whose tastes you don't know, so it's best to create an environment where people can see the possibilities for their own tastes.

Next to painting and remodeling, the most important thing you can do is reduce and remove anything that will come across as clutter. And things that are important to you may come across as "clutter" to someone else. Once you've cleaned a room, stand back and look at it with an eye to simplifying the impression it would have on somebody else. What can you remove, for now, to heighten an impression of the room being clean and orderly?

- A stack of unread or partially read books on a bedside table may look inviting to you, but it may look unattractive to others. Cut the stack to two or three.

- Three to five family photos on a shelf is better than 20.

- Pictures on the wall should be straightened and dusted.

- One or two trophy items are preferable to a dozen.

- If you have a desk, only current files should be on the desk-top, preferably in a neat stack or in a vertical file organizer; the rest should be put in file drawers or storage boxes. Aim for a clean desktop, however difficult that may be.

- Put kids' toys away when you're showing your house. If you can put them in a closet, do so. Or store them in a special box.

- Keep dirty clothes in a hamper or laundry bag and keep them off the floor.

- It's okay to store dirty dishes in the dishwasher. It's not okay to store them on the counter or in the sink.

- Cords for computers and other electronic equipment can contribute to a cluttered look. Minimize the clutter by gathering them into a bundle and securing them with a rubber band or plastic tie. Then fasten the bundle to the underside of a cabinet or table with duct tape.

- Store multiple handheld controllers in the same place, such as a small wicker basket on the coffee table.

If you can't discard it and you don't want to include it in a garage sale, make sure it's clean and presentable. This includes children's art on the refrigerator, memos on a bulletin board or wall calendar, the stack of takeout menus, and the emergency phone numbers.

Some Issues with Selling "As Is"

Rather than making extensive repairs or even doing a thorough cleaning of a house, some people elect to sell their houses in "as is" condition. This means that the buyer must accept the house in the condition presented. This approach has both pluses and minuses.

On the plus side:

- You won't have to shoulder the expense and disruption of making repairs to the foundation, the wiring, the plumbing, or wherever the problem is located.

- You can get out of the house fast, once you find a buyer.

On the minus side:

- In most states, you will have to disclose to the buyer any known problems with your house in sufficient detail to let the buyer judge whether to take on the problems.

- You will probably get a lower price for your house than if you make the repairs—sometimes a much lower price.

- Some buyers don't want the hassle of repairing other people's problems. You will probably reduce the number of potential buyers for your house.

- Unless you're quite clear about the nature and extent of the problem(s), your buyer may decide to sue you for failure to disclose the full problem after escrow closes.

Only you can evaluate whether it makes sense to sell your house in "as is" condition.

Step 5: First Impressions Count!

What sets a house apart from others on the market?

What can you do to make your house stand out from the competition?

Your house has to make a good first impression. Like dressing for a job interview, your job is to prepare your house for that first impression on a potential buyer. And as with a job interview, that means paying attention to details. Further, and again like a job interview, your house has to make a better impression than the other houses in your neighborhood that are also for sale.

This chapter is all about helping you make that good first impression.

What Else Is On the Market?

We've mentioned before that one of the most important things you can do when preparing to sell your house is to analyze the competition. We recommend using three sources:

1. From a weekend copy of the local newspaper, find houses in your neighborhood that are for sale. Drive by them. If you can, visit them during an open house to see what they're like inside.

2. Go to *www.zillow.com* and enter your address, then check out the houses for sale within your neighborhood. The red flags indicate houses that are for sale, and blue flags are "Make me move" houses where the seller is particularly eager to sell. Yellow flags indicate houses that have sold recently—note their sale prices, because they may be considerably different from the asking prices.

3. Ask a local REALTOR® about the competition. Even if you don't currently plan to list the house with a REALTOR®, a good agent will be glad to offer you an overview of what nearby houses are selling for and how yours stacks up against them. Because REALTORS® make their money by knowing what's selling and why, and what's not selling and (probably) why, they're the most likely to be able to give you tips on selling your own house.

List the Competition's Pluses and Minuses

Outside the house. When buyers drive by houses for sale in your neighborhood, what makes them want to stop and look inside? If they've driven by once, what makes them come by for a second look? For each house you drive by, rate the house on this checklist:

- What is your overall impression of the house on a scale of 1 to 10?

- How does the color compare to what else is in the neighborhood? Take off points for being the same as everything else, unless the neighborhood is in a controlled community where there appears to be a rule about colors. Also, take off points for being distinctly out of tune with the neighborhood; for instance, a purple house with yellow trim will probably not be attractive to potential buyers.

- Does the garage door color and condition complement the rest of the house?

- Does the roof appear to be in good condition, or do some shingles appear to be lifting or split?

- Is the front door and area around it inviting? A dingy front door tends to give the impression that the owners don't care about the inside either. In some neighborhoods, a red front door means that the house is warm and welcoming to visitors. This is particularly true in some Asian cultures. However, the color of the front door should go with the rest of the exterior paint scheme.

- Are the windows dirty, cracked, or broken? If so, take off points.

- How about the driveway? Take off points for dirty or broken concrete.

- Take off points for landscaping that looks dry or over-grown. (In desert areas, however, dry landscaping is a positive thing, provided that it's neat and clean.) If you can't see the windows from the street, and no fence or shrubbery has been placed deliberately to hide the house, the landscaping is overgrown.

- Does the chimney look like it's in good repair? Take off points if there isn't a spark arrestor on top of the chimney. It's inexpensive to add, but if the owner hasn't put one in, this implies that the owner hasn't thought about possible roof damage from fireplace use.

- Take off points if more than two cars are parked in the driveway. Granted, the owners may have teenagers, but extra cars may also mean that you're likely to find old cars and car parts strewn around the backyard, and they'll still be there if you buy the house. While we may have just insulted people who like to work on their cars at home, our suggestion is based on years of driving around the Bay Area every week, looking at property. We've observed that the presence of more than two cars in the driveway, particularly if some of the cars are older or rusty, usually means that somebody has been using their home as a place to repair cars and maybe sell them and that the house itself has suffered a lack of attention.

- Boats and RVs parked in the driveway detract from the salability of the house. If the owners wanted top dollar for their house, the boat or RV should have been parked somewhere else, such as a storage yard.

Inside the house. If you go inside a house, use this checklist:

- Count the number of rooms.

- Rate the quality of the paint job and other finishes and the sense of spaciousness.

- Have the kitchen and bathrooms have been updated recently?

- Could you live there? Focus on the way each room presents itself now, not on what you could do to improve it.

- Is the home energy-efficient? This can include insulation, double-pane windows, weather stripping around the doors, and other features.

- Does traffic flow smoothly from room to room?

- Are problems evident with the plumbing or wiring?

- Are the floors in decent shape? Be sure to check wood floors for warping or stains and check the carpet for wear and pet stains or odors.

How Does Your House Compare?

In general, the first thing people notice is the way your house presents itself to the street:

- Is the paint peeling or discolored?

- Does your house look dark and uninviting?

- Is the garage door askew or in disrepair?

- Does the roof look like it's old and needing replacement?

- Do the windows need replacing or cleaning?

■ If there are plants by the door, are they fresh and colorful or tired and dull?

■ Does the front yard look like it's been well maintained, or does the grass need cutting and the plants need replacing?

■ Is the driveway in good shape, or does it need repair or cleaning?

■ Are there extra cars, boats, or RVs parked in front?

Then analyze the inside of your house:

■ Does your house have more or fewer rooms than the average house in your neighborhood?

■ Is it clean—inside and out?

■ Does traffic flow well from room to room? If not, can you do something inexpensively—like move or remove some furniture—to help with traffic flow?

■ Do the rooms in your house feel bright and relaxing?

■ Does your house smell bad?

■ Would painting a room (or more) make a difference in terms of how your house compares with the competition?

■ Have you *really* gotten rid of the clutter?

Once you've compared your house against the competition, at least in terms of curb appeal, you can make a list of what you need to do to make it more attractive.

Creating Good Curb Appeal

If you're in a hurry and don't have a lot of money, concentrate on quick, inexpensive touches that will give your house a clean, uncluttered look.

- If you haven't done so already, get rid of the clutter. Your treasures and must-haves may be perceived by someone else as junk.

- Pay particular attention to how your house looks from the street. Clean up the yard and driveway. Use stain remover to clean spots from the driveway.

- Clean the windows.

- Scrape, sand, and repaint at least the front of the house, if necessary.

- Repair and repaint the garage door.

- Remove dead or dying plants and replace them with inexpensive and colorful potted plants. If you can afford them, buy a flat of flowering plants and plant them along the driveway and in front of the house. Then keep them watered.

- Trim any overgrown bushes and prune trees so that they don't hide the house.

- Consider whether a fresh coat of paint or finish would improve the appearance of your front door. You may have to sand the old finish before applying a new coat.

- If your roof looks like it's in trouble and you can't afford a new roof, consider adding an allowance in escrow to have the new owners put in a new roof.

- Move extra cars, boats, or RVs to storage.
- Move kids' toys to a side yard or inside the garage.

What's Inside the Front Door?

The next step is to analyze how your house looks once someone steps inside the front door.

- What's the first thing a visitor sees upon opening the door? If it's not going to make a pleasant impression, change it.

- Most front doors open into the living room. Stand inside the front door and look around. Does the room seem orderly and inviting? Has the furniture been arranged so that the room seems spacious yet warm? If there's a fireplace, is furniture oriented to face it, inviting cozy conversation?

- Are couches and chairs arranged in conversational groups?

- Arrange the curtains so that they let in a lot of daylight. Most buyers want to see how a room looks in daylight, so don't hide the features of your room by covering the windows.

- If you have a coffee table, don't pile a lot of magazines on it. One or two magazines is fine, or perhaps place a decorative object or maybe a couple of candles there.

- It's okay to toss a throw casually over the back of a couch, providing that the colors harmonize and the throw is in good condition. A couple of contrasting pillows also work.

- If you have a dining room, make sure it looks like a place where people gather to eat, not like the storage/office area some dining rooms become. Center the dining table under the light fixture and arrange four chairs at the table with extras against the wall. Put something colorful—a vase of flowers or a bowl of fruit—in the middle of the table.

■ In each bedroom, make sure the bed is made and clothes are off the floor, preferably in the closet. Put dresser-top items in a drawer until after the open house. Put children's toys in a toy box, a large plastic basket, or on shelves. Spray a deodorizer in any bedrooms that smell musty.

Kitchens Matter

After the initial curbside lookover and the first impression at the front door, the kitchen makes a huge impact on a potential buyer. From a five-minute tour through a house, most people will remember the kitchen, good or bad.

■ A 1950s-style tile job in a kitchen will leave a lasting impression that the house is outdated. Chipped and broken tile will give the impression that there may be water damage or dry rot under the tile.

■ Dusty or dirty cupboard doors will give the impression that the entire kitchen is dirty, as will dirt or fingerprints on the walls, door jambs, switch plates, or appliance faces.

■ Lots of small appliances, such as the toaster, coffee maker, coffee grinder, electric can opener, and blender, all on the counter, may be an expression of how you live but will detract from a sense of orderliness. For an open house, the more free counter space, the better. Unplug appliances and store them in a cupboard until the open house is over.

- Lots of people forget to sweep the kitchen floors before an open house. Don't be one of them. Be sure that your floor is spotless before potential buyers come. They'll be sure to notice the extra dog food around the bowl or the crumbs in the kick space next to the refrigerator.

- And take out the garbage. You may be used to the odor, but your potential buyer, coming in from the outside, may notice it.

Bathrooms Matter Too

We've already discussed the thorough cleaning you should do in every bathroom. If you've already cleaned thoroughly, a touch-up before potential buyers come by should be doable in fewer than five minutes, and it will make a difference.

- Swish some toilet cleaner around the toilet bowl and flush.

- Wipe out the bathroom sink and be sure to catch any dust, dirt, or shaving residue on the countertop. Clean the spout and handles.

- Check to see that the bathtub is clean and devoid of any dirty ring. Clean up any residue around the outlet and wipe down the spout and handles.

- Make sure the towels look clean and neatly folded. If you have newer towels with fresh nap, this is the time to use them.

- Spray some deodorizer in the bathrooms too.

Inexpensive Touches That Work

You can do a lot of inexpensive things to make your house more attractive. Here are a few:

- Buy several unscented candles in the same color, including votive or tea-size. (You can buy a bag of tea-size candles for under $5 at most big-box stores.) Group the bigger candles on the coffee table or on the dining room table and use the votive candles in the bathroom. If you have votive candle holders, you can use tea-size lights in them during the open house. You can also put the tea-size candles in wine goblets or other glasses. Light the candles just before prospective buyers arrive.

- Put out a plate of cookies in the kitchen. You may want to bake your own for their aroma, but be sure to put the cooking dishes in the dishwasher before people arrive.

- If agents leave their cards when they bring prospective buyers, put the cards in a small basket or bowl. That way they won't clutter the countertop.

- If you use a chlorine-based cleaner, do so well in advance of your open house. Then respray with a deodorizer to get rid of the chlorine smell.

- If you're showing your house yourself, get someone to take the kids out to play somewhere else or take them for a drive or to a movie. While it's important that your house look lived in, it's also important that visitors get a chance to experience your house without a family in it.

- Don't wash your driveway or front walk within a half hour before you expect visitors. A wet walkway may mean that people will leave muddy footprints inside your house, and washing it may also leave puddles where you don't want them. If you need to clean the driveway or walkway quickly, use a broom.

■ "Reupholster" aging throw pillows by wrapping them in colorful fabric, then pinning the ends together in the back.

■ Replace aging curtains with printed or plain-colored sheets. Run the curtain rod through the hem, hang, and tie back at the sides with pieces of ribbon.

■ Make quickie place mats from a yard of fabric cut into 12 × 18 inch pieces and frayed at the edges by pulling out some of the threads. Or turn the edges over and tape them in place with double-sided adhesive tape.

■ Make an interesting tablecloth by putting down a dark colored cloth and covering it with a square of lace. Or run contrasting colored ribbons down the middle of the table.

■ Add a decorator touch to your bed by covering it with a sheet with a pretty edge, making the bed so that the edge turns down about 12 inches, just over the top edge of a throw of a different color. Turn under the bottom edge of the throw so that it becomes a wide color stripe across the middle of the bed. Plump the sleeping pillows and arrange a throw pillow or two in the middle.

8

Step 6: Staging Your House

More and more home sellers are staging their homes in an attempt to get the best possible price.

Should you stage your house?

You're ready to put your house on the market. You've cleaned it thoroughly and either gotten rid of or stored many things that might otherwise detract from the house's appearance. The house feels a little bare to you, but at least it's clean and orderly. Now what can you do?

Your Neat Stuff May Be Someone Else's Turnoff

We've said before that when selling your house, you need to distinguish between what you like to live with and what will help your house appeal to potential buyers.

Suppose, for instance, that you happen to love the idea of living in a fairy-tale castle. You have decorated nooks and crannies with pictures and objects, and your walls have a fanciful paint job. Someone else is likely to find it difficult to see beyond your decorations to picture what they could do to make it their own space.

Or suppose you love the gothic look and live in a house with lots of black touches. Most potential buyers will recoil at all that black and not give your house more than a cursory look.

Or suppose you just love living in a cute, country-style home, and you have painted flowers or homey slogans on the walls and put gingham curtains and chintz upholstery everywhere. Again, this is too much information for most potential buyers, who may run like scared rabbits from your country haven.

Even stark, modernistic themes can turn off buyers. A home that's all straight lines, cubical furniture, and monotones without any comfy touches, such as pillows or throws, can feel cold and uninviting to a potential buyer.

The Clean, Uncluttered Look

The best impression your house can give is the product of an environment that is clean and orderly while also warm and inviting. You want your house to look something like the model homes in new construction areas.

The catch is, of course, that you probably don't have a lot of money to spend and you probably have to work with the furniture you have.

The Power of Paint

If you can afford the time and the expense, one of the cheapest ways to improve the look of a room is to apply a fresh coat of paint. Aim for a neutral color but one that makes the room feel bright and relaxing.

Choosing the right paint color can make a huge difference in how the room appears to a potential buyer. For living area walls, choose a light neutral color that will appeal to a lot of people. Twenty years ago, everybody was choosing off-white; these days, people are looking for slightly warmer tones, such as light tan or other natural colors.

Bedroom colors can pick up the colors of bed linens or complement a piece of furniture that is a primary focus in the room. Don't use strong colors in a house that's for sale—buyers frequently have a problem visualizing themselves in a room that makes a strong statement.

Bathrooms can use stronger colors, provided that they complement facial tones. Lavender, for instance, tends to gray out facial colors. Blue tones do too. Warmer colors like coral, light orange, yellow, gold, and tan tend to warm up skin tones.

Ideally, the most work in painting a room is involved in preparation. Move all of the furniture out of the room, if possible, and cover the floor with a plastic tarp, newspapers, or old sheets. Use blue painter's tape to cover areas that won't get painted this time, such as window trim, door jambs, and baseboards.

When you paint, use a good roller for the walls and at least a medium-quality brush for corners and edges. Carefully remove painter's tape while the paint is still wet but wait till the paint is dry to to remove any tarps.

Moving the Furniture Back

Before moving your stuff back into the room, take a look at the empty room. This is your opportunity to stage the room by bringing back only those pieces that will add to the inviting feel you're after. Yes, you have to live there until the house is sold, but do you really need three couches and a couple of chairs?

Is there a better way to hide the clutter associated with the TV set and all of the other electronic gear? Also, piles of books on the floor may make your house feel lived in, but they actually detract from the appearance of orderliness.

In children's rooms, one good way to deal with all those toys on the floor is to stack inexpensive plastic crates against a wall and store the toys there. Another solution is to buy an inexpensive bookcase, paint it a bright color that goes with the rest of the room, and store the toys on the shelves.

Clear the Counters

Counters must be clean. Clear off and either dispose of or hide all those magazines, papers, or baskets of small things you like to keep handy. This is especially true of kitchen and bathroom counters. Put away small appliances—yes, that includes the toaster in the kitchen and the hair dryer in the bathroom—and make sure the countertops are sparkling clean. Your buyers aren't interested in how you live. They're interested in how *they* will live in your house.

Brighter Is Better

We're talking about lighting, of course. Dim lights are great for setting a mood in the evening, but they detract from selling a house. Turn on all the lights in a room and decide whether they add to the room's livability. If having them all on is too much, selectively turn one or two off at a time.

For seniors especially, it's better to have too much light than too little, as senior eyesight tends to diminish with age, especially night vision. Reading lights help a lot.

In the kitchen, well-lit workspaces are especially appreciated. Stand at a counter and observe where shadows fall. If work areas are in shadow, consider adding some inexpensive under-counter lights—they can run as little as $10 at home stores.

What's That Smell?

Nothing turns off people as much as odd smells in a house. That means no pet scents, no stale cooking smells, and in particular, no cigarette smoke odors.

If you have a cat litter box, change it the day before your house is to be open to buyers. And if your house is being shown by agents who can bring buyers by unexpectedly, change the litter box every day.

If you have pet odors in the carpet, use an enzyme spray specifically designed to remove the odors. Spray everywhere there have been pet accidents. You may need several applications for a single spot. If you can shampoo the carpets and remove some of the odor, do so.

Some food gives off unpleasant odors while cooking, particularly fish and members of the cabbage family. Air out the house, particularly the room where food odors collect.

Smoke from cigarettes and cigars can be insidious: it seeps into and remains with carpets, upholstery, and drapes long after the smoker has left the room. It even clings to painted walls. With the number of smokers in the United States dropping every year, it pays to assume that potential buyers will find the smell of stale smoke offensive. If your house smells of smoke, use one of the upholstery sprays liberally and frequently to counter the smell. And by the way, a fresh coat of paint usually covers up the smoke smell on a wall.

While you may believe that the chlorine smell from some cleansers or the smell of products like Lysol and air fresheners helps your house smell fresh and clean, most buyers don't really like it. Nothing beats the smell of fresh air in a house.

Some real estate agents now believe that the smell of freshly baked bread or cookies, cinnamon potpourri, or scented candles actually detracts from the impression a house gives.

The Power of Fresh

Don't overdo it, but bouquets of fresh flowers—on the dining room table, on the coffee table, or on the fireplace mantle or in small bunches in the bathroom or the master bedroom—can give a fresh, perky feel to a house.

A bowl of fresh fruit—particularly all of one color—can be used when you can't get fresh flowers.

Green plants also can give a feeling of bringing the freshness of outdoors inside. Because most people don't associate green plants with "clutter," you can put a potted plant on a countertop or a windowsill to improve the appearance of a room.

"Professional" Staging

If the thought of staging your home yourself just overwhelms you, consider hiring a professional. Some of these stagers are real estate agents who stage houses they list as an additional service; some may be interior decorators who do staging as a part of their design business.

West Coast REALTOR® Barb Schwarz believes that staging speeds up sales in a sluggish market and can bump up prices 2 percent to 10 percent in a moderate market. The biggest advantage occurs with luxury homes or in a market with bidding wars over properties, where effective staging can boost prices by 20 percent to 50 percent, she says.

Professional stagers have their own props and furniture or can rent what's necessary, and their services can cost around $100 an hour. Staging a small house can take as little as three hours; staging a large and expensive house can take several days, depending on what the sellers decide to do. In most cases, the cost of staging is paid by the seller, though in some cases, it is paid by the seller's agent as part of the listing commission.

9

Step 7: Alternative Marketing

Normal marketing measures work when you're in a normal market. In today's market, however, "normal" usually doesn't work.

Standard Stuff: Using the MLS, Open Houses, and More

Most realtors tend to rely on established means of marketing a house. They'll list the property on the MLS, put up a sign at the house with fliers, feed information from the flyers to their personal website and their brokerage's site, place ads in the local papers (usually via their brokerage), and hold open houses. Depending on the circumstances, they might also hire someone to put out fliers or wave a signboard on a public street. Basically, the agent puts out the word and waits for someone to get back. And that's the extent of the standard marketing package.

Using Alternative Marketing

Alternative marketing approaches start from a fundamentally different assumption. If you're going to put out the word, put out the word where interested, motivated buyers are more likely to be. Go to where the people who are interested in spending money are actually located. List your property in an environment that is populated with willing buyers, not just a large number of sellers.

There is, however, an important caveat to using alternative marketing approaches. While you, the owner, are directly working these approaches, you may also need to coordinate with your realtor.

Community Papers

Putting ads in local community papers often produces a better crop of possible buyers, for the simple reason that you are specifically targeting the community in which you're trying to sell. This means that you're talking to the people who are already in the community and already interested in what's going on there. Quite often, you will find buyers who are interested in your home.

Internet Pages

Putting up a website for your house is becoming a very common thing, especially for higher-end houses. The key thing to understand when going this route is that if you build a website, it needs to be attractive and professional looking. To get an idea of what that looks like, check with some of your local realtors. Or even just drive around the neighborhood, looking at other houses for sale—you'll be surprised how many of them sprout website addresses these days.

You also need to understand that a website in and of itself isn't a magic wand that will bring in a buyer. It's really nothing more than an electronic brochure that someone can easily look at. That said, a website for your house can be very helpful when you use one or more of the following strategies, because it allows you to publish the same information once (to the website) and reuse that information in other places that link directly to your website.

eBay. eBay (*www.ebay.com*) is an interesting place to list real estate. While it is inherently an environment that will bring you only willing buyers, the disparity between a national-level online auction forum and individual state real estate laws means that you must be careful in how you approach listing your property on eBay. The primary areas of concern are these:

■ Because you're probably using a conventional listing via a realtor and MLS listing, you need to make sure that your ad allows for the possibility of getting an offer through conventional channels.

■ You also need to provide for dealing with financing conditions, inspections, title insurance, and escrow issues.

■ Make sure that the legal forms are followed for your state. Depending on the circumstances, this may mean that you can only list the auction as a "right to offer" auction, rather than directly auctioning full title to the property.

If you decide you want to list your property on eBay, you should review other real estate ads from your state to get an idea of the legally required structure for an auction of your property. It would also be a good idea to have either your agent handle the actual listing or, if you handle it, involve your realtor in the process of drafting the actual text of the listing and in dealing with any potential buyers who respond.

Craigslist. Craigslist (*www.craiglist.com*) started life as a referral list in San Francisco, passing for-sale ads, tips, and community information around. Since then, it has grown into an international forum with a variety of specialty sections—including assorted real estate sections.

Craigslist is organized by geographic area with hotlinks for virtually every major city in the United States and Canada, plus state and national links. Within any given geographic area, Craigslist provides local links for real estate listings, allowing you to target your specific area.

What's the point of using a site like Craigslist? Fundamentally, it's self-screening. The only people who will contact you are people who are already interested in your property and, if you write a descriptive ad, are at least theoretically prequalified for the terms you're seeking for your house.

Craigslist has some of the same issues as a listing location that eBay does, in that you need to involve your realtor in the listing process and in drafting the text of your proposed ad. Make sure that you include all the key words that you think are important to describe your house and your situation. You might be surprised at the number of people who search through Craigslist listings for specific types of properties.

One other issue you should be aware of, based on our experience with Craigslist, is that you can expect a certain number of "tire kickers"—people who aren't really serious about buying but who still want to look. Screening these people takes some time, but you should regard it as an inherent part of the process. What we've found works in such a situation is to ask them to drive by the property and, based on that, respond if they're still interested. It's a simple, low-effort way to get through these people and find out if they're serious.

Zillow. We introduced Zillow in Chapter 3 as a home valuation tool. You can also use it as a marketing tool. Zillow includes an option to list a home for sale, either as an agent or as the owner: See *www.zillow.com/postings/Postings.htm*.

The nice thing about Zillow is that it allows you to expand on a wide variety of information that's already available about your house. You can, for example, include digital pictures of the inside of your home, add more information, and use the valuation tools to get a realistic idea of what the houses in your neighborhood are actually selling for.

Company bulletin boards. Depending on where you work, you may have access to internal company bulletin boards or newsletters that allow you to list information of interest to other employees. Putting a listing on your bulletin board or in your newsletter is an easy, quick way to get your house in front of people in your area who might be looking for a new house.

Relocation offices. Quite a few larger companies work cooperatively with realtors to provide relocation services. Contact them directly to let them know that you have a house that you are motivated to sell and that you are willing to work with potential buyers. It's an easy and quick way to get access to more potential buyers.

There are two relatively easy ways to find these offices:

1. Ask your realtor, or the broker who runs your agent's office, if the firm has contacts with the local relocation assistance offices for the larger companies in your area. If you use this approach, you should probably have your realtor make the contact with the office rather than doing so directly.

2. Search the Internet for "relocation assistance" and the nearest large city. You will probably have to sort through the results that you get, but you should find a number of possible contacts as a result.

I Know Someone Who . . .

One of the oldest tricks in the book, but one that most people nonetheless overlook, is the game of "I know someone who . . ."—also known as your friends and family. Putting out the word among the people you know can yield surprising results. This is often even easier if you're set up electronically, so that if a friend says he knows someone who's interested, you can easily send him the URL of your website so he has more information.

Integrating Your Efforts with Those of Your Realtor

If you are working with a realtor, then before you start using alternative marketing methods, make sure that you and your realtor are coordinating your mutual efforts.

10

Step 8:
Creative Financing

Sometimes it takes more than a good price and an attractive house and yard to make a sale. What can you can do to make financing more flexible?

Being Prepared for Financing Options

Look at what you're offering for sale with your house.

- Do you need to get cash out of your house, perhaps to buy another house or to pay off a divorce settlement? If you don't, perhaps you can offer to take back part of your equity in the form of a second—or even third—mortgage. Be careful that you don't have more than about 85 percent of the house's value in loans, however, so that you have a cushion in case market values in your neighborhood go down or if you have to foreclose on the buyers.

- Are you assuming that your buyer will come up with all new financing? If not, what kinds of attractive financing options do you believe you can offer? Several options are explained later in this chapter.

■ What is the lending market like at the moment? Is it easy to qualify for an 80 percent loan-to-value loan? If not, what can you do to help a potential buyer qualify for a loan? If your buyer can qualify for a 70 percent loan and if you can offer to help with secondary financing, such as taking back a 10–20 percent second mortgage, perhaps with interest-only payments and a balloon payment at the end of two years, would that help your buyer?

■ If the buyer has other real estate, you may be able to take some sort of secondary loan on the other property to make up the full sale price of your property. For instance, if the buyer also owns a vacation property on a lake and it already has a 70 percent loan, you may be able to take a 10 percent second mortgage on the lake property as partial payment for your house. Be careful, however, that the buyer will be able to make the loan payments on your house as well as the loan payments on the other property.

If the lending market is very expensive or not many people are able to qualify for loans, consider some of the other options explained in this chapter.

Offering Rebates for Problems You Can't Fix

If your house has major problems—such as cracks in the foundation from settling, major plumbing or electrical problems, or a roof that needs replacement—and you can't afford to fix the problems, consider offering your buyer some sort of financial allowance as part of the final package.

For instance, suppose your roof was damaged in a storm and your insurance won't pay enough to fix it. If you have a buyer who's willing to work with you, you might offer the buyer the amount the insurance company will pay plus the difference in return for accepting the roof as it is. You will have to initiate the claim with your insurance company, but your buyer can facilitate the repairs. When the repairs are complete, you must hand over the insurance payment to the buyer.

Or suppose you have discovered a leak in the plumbing under your house that has caused some damage to the subfloor under a toilet. A contractor has told you that you'll need to remove the toilet and replace the subfloor and possibly supporting beams in that bathroom, and you can't afford to pay for it now. By acknowledging the problem up front to a buyer and offering a reasonable amount in escrow to fix the problem, you make sure the problem isn't the buyer's problem.

Lease/Options

If you haven't been able to sell your house and you really need to move on, consider a lease/option. This can at least help you cover the mortgage payments, taxes, and insurance on your house while giving a potential buyer the right to buy the house eventually. In a tight lending market, it may be a good way to unload your house, but it won't give you much immediate cash from your equity.

A *lease/option* arrangement means that you're giving someone the right to lease your property for a fixed period of time, usually a year or more, with an option to buy the property at a price you agree upon up front. Normally the tenants pay a certain amount of money up front for the right to buy the property, and sometimes that *option money* is considered part of the purchase price. Sometimes some percentage of the lease payments can be credited against the purchase price too.

For instance, suppose someone wants to buy your house but can't afford to do so until their own house sells. You might offer this potential buyer a lease option with monthly lease payments of $1,500 (which covers the monthly cost of your mortgage, taxes, and insurance) and a $5,000 option to buy your house within one year. If, at the end of the year, the buyer decides to exercise the option, you don't have to credit the $5,000 toward the purchase price unless you agreed to do so in the written contract; the $5,000 then becomes the price the buyer paid for keeping the house off the market. On the other hand, crediting the $5,000 toward the purchase price gives the buyer more incentive to finish the purchase.

Property Exchanges

We'll go into more detail about exchanges in Chapter 11, but briefly, a property exchange, commonly called a *1031 exchange*, involves exchanging one piece of property—or a set of properties—for another. The *1031* refers to the section of the IRS tax code that covers the rules for such an exchange and outlines the way property can be exchanged without incurring tax penalties. If any cash is part of the transaction, you have to pay taxes on that part.

Exchanging property is a popular specialty within real estate, allowing you to dispose of one property and get another.

Refinance and Hold or Rent

If you find that you simply can't sell your house right now, consider refinancing it and renting it out. If your house has appreciated and comparable sales support a higher market value, you may be able to borrow more of the equity than you now have.

For instance, suppose you have a house that was worth $300,000 two years ago and you have an 80 percent loan-to-value mortgage of $240,000. You have an equity of 20 percent, or $60,000. Now suppose that your house has appreciated 10 percent over the last two years and currently has a market value of $330,000. You now have an equity of $60,000 plus the additional $30,000 of appreciated value, or $90,000.

You have two options here: refinance the first mortgage or add a second mortgage.

Option 1: Refinance the First Mortgage

This option is particularly attractive if you currently have an adjustable mortgage rate that is due to increase shortly. By replacing the existing first mortgage with another first mortgage—preferably with a fixed rate of interest—you can pull out some equity and avoid the bombshell of vastly increased payments when the interest rate adjusts. Just how much you'll be able to pull out will depend on the current interest rate offered by the new lender and what prepayment penalties the current lender will charge. Once you've done that, you can rent out the house.

Suppose you have a 30-year adjustable rate mortgage (ARM) of $240,000 and your current interest is 6 percent, making your monthly mortgage payment $1,194.03. The contract with your lender says that the interest rate will jump to 11 percent as of March 1, 2008, resulting in monthly payments of $2,180.02. If you refinance before January 2010, you'll have to pay a $20,000 prepayment penalty. Is it worth refinancing to a new fixed-rate mortgage? Here's how to compare:

Your current mortgage is for	$240,000.00
over	30 years
at an annual interest rate of	6%
and monthly payments of	$1,194.03

Assuming your house has appreciated 10 percent since you got the current mortgage two years ago, here's how you can calculate whether you should refinance:

Your house is now worth	$330,000.00
and an 80 percent loan at a fixed rate of 6.5 percent will get you a mortgage of	$264,000.00
over	30 years
at an annual interest rate of	6.5%
with monthly payments of	$1,443.88
If you pay off the existing mortgage now, with a new fixed rate mortgage, you'll still owe (assuming you've made 24 payments on the loan)	−$179,115.16
plus the prepayment penalty,	−$20,000.00
or	−$199,115.16
That leaves a balance payable to you in cash of about	$64,884.84
and a difference in monthly payments of	$249.85

These figures are not exact, because you'll also have to pay points and closing costs, which will vary from lender to lender. And of course, you'll still be paying insurance premiums and property taxes.

Option 2: Take Out a New Second Mortgage

Another option is to take out a new second mortgage, tapping more of the new equity, while you rent out the house. Let's start by assuming you have already converted your adjustable rate mortgage to a fixed-rate mortgage. You have the following:

a current mortgage of	$240,000
over	30 years
at an annual interest rate of	6%
and monthly payments of	$1,194.03

You know the value of your house is now $330,000, so you have $90,000 in equity. If you borrow up to 80 percent of the loan-to-value, you have the following:

Your current market value is	$330,000
and 80 percent of that is	$264,000
Therefore, you can borrow another	$24,000
as a second mortgage, for	2
years, at an annual interest rate of	12%
with interest-only payments each month of	$240
and the full principal of $24,000 will be due at the end of two years.	

Let's compare the options:

	Option 1	Option 2
New principal	$264,000	$240,000
		+ 24,000
		$264,000
Old payments	$1,194.03	$1,194.03
New payments	$1,443.88	$1,194.03
		+ 240.00
		$1,434.03
Cash you get	$64,884.84	$24,000.00

Duh!

Sales Contracts

If you have buyers but they can't get financing, one alternative is to draft a sale contract directly. In today's real estate market, this approach is more common than you might realize. We had one transaction where the buyers were preapproved by their lender for the property, yet we ultimately had to write our own sales contract after the lender walked away rather than go through with writing the mortgage. This approach is most effective when you have a fair amount of equity in your property and need a way to get around balky financing issues to make your transaction work.

If you decide to write a sales contract, negotiate the terms of your agreement, then have your real estate agent draft the language of the contract or have a real estate lawyer write up the agreement. As a rule, you want to write the contract rather than allow the buyer to write it—arguing over a contract that the buyer writes and tries to impose on you when you're trying to close a sale is never very pleasant, from our experience.

Wrappers

One trick we've used on occasion is to write a wrapper around an existing first mortgage as a means of getting a sale to close. (A wrapper is a note that keeps the existing mortgage in place—along with the seller's responsibility to keep up payments on it—but requires to buyer to make the payments plus whatever additional payments the seller requires. Wrappers may not be legal in some states.) What this does is create a junior note that subsumes the existing first mortgage. You will have to deal with a few issues if you decide to go this route, but you can determine if these are in fact issues and work them out ahead of time by examining your existing loan documents. The most important issues you need to resolve are these:

- If there is a due-on-sale clause in your existing first mortgage, you must get written authorization from the lender to waive this clause and allow you to issue a wrapper.

- If there is a prohibition against junior notes, you must get a written waiver from the lender to issue the wrapper.

- If there is a prohibition or penalties against early payoffs in the first mortgage, then you must make sure to include the same prohibition or penalties in your wrapper.

In general, if you plan to issue a wrapper, make certain that you involve a real estate lawyer in drafting your contract and documents.

Wrappers are, in general, a good way to make a sale of a difficult property go through if you have a lot of equity and closing is proving difficult. While the wrapper exists, you receive payment on it as with any other loan. In addition, if you want to get cash out of your wrapper, there is an active market in second mortgages, though you should be aware that you will probably have to accept a significant discount to cash out of your note early.

Assumable Financing

One way to make a sale happen is to arrange for assumable financing. Under most mortgage contracts, lenders have a *due-on-sale clause,* which requires that the loan be paid off when the property is sold. However, many lenders are willing at least to consider allowing new purchasers to assume existing loans. They usually require some form of prequalification before allowing this kind of assumption, however, so your buyer may have to go through the lender's qualification process.

That being said, and depending on the circumstances, your lender may be quite willing to grant an approval, if it gets even pro forma proof that the payments on the loan will be made. Why? Because banks and lenders need performing loans in their portfolios to stay in business. Just about anything that will give them that is, thus, worth pursuing. Basically, you need to start from the principle of "They can't say yes if you don't ask." Ask! Even if you and your agent feel pessimistic about the odds, you might be surprised.

Short Sales

One of the big last-ditch sales options is called a short sale. It's used when you need to sell a property and you have more debt on the property than you can sell it for. If you are in a situation where you need to sell your house, and you're less concerned about getting something after escrow closes, then a short sale might be just the thing for you.

A *short sale*, just so you understand the term, is when you sell the house for less than the total of the loans and liens on the property. As a result, you won't see a penny from the transaction—guaranteed. That is, unfortunately, the nature of the beast.

The primary item that you will need to make a short sale work is the approval of the lender or lenders who hold your mortgages, plus anyone else who has a lien against you (a state or federal tax lien, for example, for back taxes). You'll also almost certainly need to have a real estate agent working with you, because lenders tend not to like short sales where an accredited agent isn't involved, though they have been known to accept them if either the buyer or the seller is otherwise professionally qualified.

Assuming you have an offer but it's below what you would otherwise need to pay off everything, what you need to do is for you *and* your agent to contact the appropriate lenders and lien holders and get their authorization in writing for a short sale. Once you have those authorizations, you can go ahead and close escrow.

The effects of a short sale will vary depending on the circumstances. However, you can use the following rules of thumb:

- Loans against your house will be paid off, and you will owe nothing further.

- Liens that have been filed against your property will probably follow you around. If they are partially paid off, then you will still be responsible for the balance, unless the lien holder agrees to release your liability.

If you are thinking of using a short sale, discuss the matter with your real estate agent—or the agent's broker if your agent doesn't have much experience dealing with short sales. Make *certain* that whoever is representing you during the sale has access to short-sale experience. Trying to do a short sale when nobody's ever done one before can be a very painful experience.

Step 9:
Exchanging

If you consider your house an investment property, you may be able to take advantage of special tax maneuvers that let you exchange one property for another without incurring taxes.

The IRS lets you exchange business or investment property for other business or investment property of a like kind. This provision may apply to your house if you can demonstrate that it is a business or investment property, even if you're living in it.

Under IRS code section 1031, if you exchange one property for another like it, you don't have to pay income or capital gains taxes on the gain in value until you actually receive money or dissimilar property. If, as part of the exchange, you also receive other dissimilar property or money, you pay taxes on the gain to the extent of the other property and money received. This lets you sell and buy property of like kind while deferring tax consequences.

A successful 1031 exchange allows you to reinvest 100 percent of the equity from the sale of a property into the purchase of another property without recognizing any gain. You can do this type of property sale and reinvestment either through a simultaneous or delayed exchange. In a delayed exchange, you have 45 days from the close of escrow on your property to identify another property as a like-kind replacement property, and you must close escrow on the replacement property within 180 days.

In most cases, a 1031 exchange is done as three-party delayed exchange also known as a "Starker exchange," where a third party facilitates transfer of both properties and provides a "safe harbor" against transfer of money. In a delayed exchange, actual title transfer doesn't occur until all the properties involved are in escrow. Doing this process correctly is extremely important, or the IRS may consider it a taxable event.

The advantages of an exchange are that you may be able to "sell" your house by exchanging it for two or more investment properties, then sell one or both of them when it's appropriate for you. This approach works really well when you have an expensive house that hasn't sold and you find two or more less-expensive properties that, combined, are close to the value of your expensive house.

If the value of your house, minus any loans or liens, is less than the value of what you're being offered, you will have to add either property to match the value you're being offered or an equivalent amount of cash. If the value of your house is more than the value of what you're being offered, the other party must make up the difference, and if it's in cash, you'll have to pay the taxes on the difference.

Finding a Viable Exchange

There are two fundamental rules to identifying a replacement property in a tax-deferred exchange:

1. The total purchase price of the replacement like-kind property must be equal to or greater than the total net sales price of the relinquished real estate property.

2. All the equity received from the sale of the relinquished real estate property must be used to acquire the replacement like-kind property.

IRS section 1031 requires the exchanger to identify the replacement property within 45 days from the close of the sale property, even if the 45th day falls on a Saturday, Sunday, or official U.S. holiday. The exchanger has a remaining 135 days to close on the replacement property. These combined dates may total no more than 180 days (6 months).

A number of websites offer advice and/or listings of exchange properties. There are also local, regional, and national meetings of exchangers where anybody can find out about the real estate exchange process and explore possible exchange properties. Many of the participants at these meetings come prepared to make deals on the spot.

Tax Implications

Because there are IRS rules regarding the timing of real estate exchanges, the type of property that can be exchanged, and just what qualifies for an exchange, it's wise to get your accountant involved if you're thinking about a 1031 exchange. Most exchanges involve simply exchanging equity in one property for the same equity in another, but sometimes the transactions can get complex. An accountant experienced in 1031 exchanges can tell you about possible complications and their tax implications.

The basic rule of thumb in a 1031 is that if you get cash out of the exchange, you have to pay taxes on it. However, if you wind up with two or more properties, you may be able to get cash out without immediately paying taxes on it.

Getting Cash Out of the Deal

One of the most common ways to get cash out of an exchange is when one of the properties involved can be refinanced.

If you refinance your property before you exchange it, you get to keep the cash, although you'll have less equity to exchange. Depending on whether you have enough expenses to offset the gain, you may or may not be able to avoid paying taxes on the gain. Discuss this with your accountant.

If you refinance the property you're acquiring after the exchange, the cash is yours, and you won't incur taxes until you sell or otherwise dispose of the property.

12

Step 10: Auctions

Auctions are a simple, time-tested way of finding out what something is really worth—which may, or may not, match up with your expectations.

Real estate auctions have, of late, enjoyed a resurgence of interest. Why? Because they're a straightforward way of finding the maximum reasonable price that potential purchasers are willing to pay.

One thing that most people don't realize is that the classic "multiple offers with counters" type of real estate sales negotiation is, in fact, a slow-motion auction. You're doing pretty much the same thing: accepting bids and allowing the price to "float up" to the natural selling price of a property.

Types of Auctions

Generally speaking, there are three types of auctions:

1. *Minimum bid auctions* have a set minimum price that is publicly stated prior to the auction. Minimum bid auctions tend to produce fewer, better-qualified bidders. The minimum bid tends to discourage bidders (because less possibility of an amazing deal is perceived), but because they know the minimum price coming in the door, all bidders know what they are getting into.

2. *Reserve auctions* do not require a minimum bid per se, but they have a reserve price that is held between the seller and the auctioneer. Generally speaking, in a reserve auction, you have the option of rejecting any and all bids, especially those that do not meet the reserve price. However, if the reserve price is met, you will owe the auctioneer a commission, regardless of whether you actually accept the auction price.

3. *Absolute auctions* are the classic auction you think of when you have competing bidders raising each other. Generally, absolute auctions require a minimum bid of some sort. Auctioneers conducting absolute auctions often charge a fee, which is chargeable against their commission, to cover the expenses involved in putting on the auction.

There are, of course, variations on these basic types, but they all derive from these three. A *sealed-bid auction*, for example, allows as many bidders as are interested to submit sealed bids for a particular property. All bids are then opened at an appointed time, and the winning bid is accepted. Many governmental agencies use sealed-bid auctions to dispose of surplus property.

Benefits of Auctions

Auctions offer a number of benefits over regular listing practices:

- They provide a firm deadline for when the property will be sold, which you can't get when you list a property.

- They are a good way to determine value of a property that might otherwise be difficult to value.

- They tend to produce a bit of focus in the market through more intensive marketing.

Finding the Right Auctioneer
Versus Doing It Yourself

Broadly speaking, most states only allow two possible categories of auctioneers: the actual owner of a property (you) or a licensed auctioneer.

Auctioneers bring many of the same benefits to the table in an auction that a licensed real estate agent does when you list your property. Highest among these are professional expertise, detailed knowledge of the auction process, and knowledge of the legal requirements for conducting an auction.

That doesn't mean that you can't conduct an auction yourself. A gentleman we recently met (let's call him John) conducted his own auction, marketing and showing the property and dealing with all the issues on his own. In John's case, he opted to conduct a sealed-bid auction, with a minimum bid set at about 75 percent of what he thought the house was worth—just enough to cover his mortgage. After marketing the auction for three weeks, when it came time to sell, John received a total of four bids, with the best coming in about 11% above his minimum.

That being said, there are quite a few auctioneers out there qualified to handle a real estate auction, so finding them is generally not that difficult. Searching the Internet for "real estate auction" plus your state will probably give you leads almost immediately. However, having done so, you might do well to perform a little extra background research and verify the auctioneer's credentials. Some auction groups seem to have a distressing tendency to wind up in court on a regular basis, and we can't recommend patronizing them.

Publicizing Your Auction

Once you've set up your auction, you need to publicize it. If you are using an auctioneer, generally that person will publicize the auction as part of the normal course of business, putting out newsletters, advertising, flyers, and calendaring their auction on a website. You should probably follow up with them, however, to make sure that (a) your house looks good in the advertising and (b) that the publicity about your house is actually getting out there. Don't be distressed if your house is bundled with others into a group auction, however. This is common practice and usually brings in more bidders.

If you're going to auction your own home, then you've got a bit more work on your hands. The following seem to be good places to advertise your auction:

- Create a website showing your house to its best advantage. This doesn't have to be extremely fancy but just something to get the facts out there. You should, however, put the auction terms clearly on the website so that potential buyers make no mistake about what they are.

- Prepare a flyer that shows off your house and describes the auction and its timing and terms clearly. You can reuse this.

- Send copies of the flyer to all of the local real estate agents for which you can find addresses in case they have potential buyers.

- Putting up signage around your neighborhood and on the nearby main thoroughfares *with the property address* is a good idea. Remember John's auction, above? That's how we found out about it—because of one of his signs.

- Put ads in the local papers, both in the community papers and, if you can afford it, in the larger regional paper. If they're filed electronically, include a link to your website.

■ Keep an ad on Craigslist. Make sure it's in your local real estate section. You will probably have to refile the ad about once a week, because Craigslist automatically cycles off ads after seven days. You can also have this ad point to your website.

Preparing for an Auction

Regardless of whether you decide to auction your property yourself or go with an established auctioneer, you must make sure that your auction complies with all relevant state and local real estate transaction requirements. We strongly suggest that if you do not use an established auctioneer, you sit down with either an experienced real estate agent who has dealt with auctions or a real estate lawyer to put your auction package together. Among the items in your package should have are the following:

■ *Where, when, and what type of auction.* Make sure that all of the auction terms are clearly spelled out. If there's going to be a minimum bid, clearly spell that out.

■ *The auction contract.* Many auction-listing services have complete copies of their contracts as part of their listings on their websites. Don't be afraid to make use of good contract language that someone else wrote. Purely as an example, Interstate Auction of Virginia (*www. interstateauctionva.com*) includes the terms of each auction directly on the auction Web page.

■ *Full disclosure about your property.* This should include any legal encumbrances that may exist (mortgages, liens, development restrictions, and so forth). Failure to disclose fully information about your property can result in a failed sale, a quick trip to court, or both.

Overall, we can't really think of any reason not to include a real estate professional who is knowledgeable about auctions in at least this portion of the process. The reason is simple: there are too many potential legal loopholes and ways to get into trouble not to make sure you are legally covered. That said, as noted previously, you don't necessarily have to use a professional auctioneer. Just make sure that, if you aren't using an auctioneer, you have some form of legal assistance in putting together your paperwork.

Qualifying Bidders

Generally speaking, you want to have *qualified bidders* for your property. What that means when you're talking about real estate is that you want the buyer to have the financial means to consummate the sale of your property once the auction is completed. Generally this takes the form of two requirements:

1. *Completing a bidder registration form.* This requires complete contact and financial information.

2. *Providing certified funds at the time of registration.* Usually this is an amount of from 1 percent to 5 percent of the expected sale price of the property (depending on the property). These funds are held until returned at close of bidding.

If you are using an auctioneer, make sure that they have bidder qualification procedures in place and that they follow those procedures.

Legal Issues

As we've noted, a number of legal issues are involved in conducting a real estate auction. If you decide not to use a professional auctioneer, we cannot stress enough that you should utilize the services of a real estate lawyer in drafting your sales contract. Among local, state, and federal requirements, the legal pitfalls involved can be simply enormous, easily involving the entire price of your house and more. Among the issues that you will need to address in setting up your auction are these:

- The name of the legal title holder or holders

- A valid legal description of the property being sold

- The duties and compensation of the auctioneer

- The duties of the seller (obtaining survey, title report, and a listing/description of any personal property included in the sale)

- The duration of the auction contract

- Whether the auction will be reserve, minimum bid, or absolute

- Any items required to meet local, state, and federal law

The auction contract should be clear about how the property will be marketed, including information on advertising, times for showing the property to prospective buyers, and the location and time of the auction. It should also detail whether the seller pays for any of the costs incurred, over the actual bid price. A good auction contract should also include the development of a bidder's information package, including the actual sales contract to be executed with the successful bidder, financing information, all of the terms of the auction, and any information about extra expenses associated with owning the property (homeowners' association dues, for example).

Auction listing agreements are generally more complicated than the exclusive listing agreements used in conventional sales of real estate, because many of the "we can deal with that later" issues that crop up in listing agreements have to be dealt with in advance with an auction contract.

You should also note that you have an absolute right to cancel an auction right up until the opening of bids. You must do so in a clear manner, however, and before bidding begins.

For a truly exhaustive treatment of real estate auction legal issues, we cannot recommend highly enough the article at this website: *http://findarticles.com/p/articles/mi_qa3714/is_200601/ai_n17184222/pg_1*. Beware, though—it's 31 pages of tightly packed legal discussion.

Perils and Pitfalls

■ Before going into an auction, you should understand that sales talk from the auctioneer is just that—talk. It is not a guarantee, and it may well set your expectations unrealistically high.

■ Understand that you may not necessarily get the price you want from your auction, and depending on the auction format that you've chosen, you may be stuck with that price.

■ If you have a reserve bid or minimum bid auction, you have reserved the right to refuse all bids if they don't meet a certain minimum price level. If you are using an absolute or no-reserve auction format, however, you are legally obligated to accept the highest bid, no matter what it is.

■ Because real estate auctions for nondistressed (foreclosure, etc.) properties are a relatively new phenomenon for residential sales, legal and ethical rules are still catching up. Here, more than anywhere, getting a second opinion is critical. Having a real estate attorney or other real estate contract professional review your auctioneer's proposed contract is quite important.

■ Make sure that you review what the auctioneer says about a reasonable price that you can expect both against what other homes are selling for in your area and against the auctioneer's previous performance.

Here's an example of how important this can be: A family agreed to auction their property. The auctioneer verbally told the family that their property would bring in $850,000 at auction. On that basis, the family signed the contract, even though the contract specifically disclaimed the auctioneer's representations about the property. When it came time to sell the property, the seller was concerned because only five bidders showed up and they were ready to cancel. To soothe the seller's nerves, the auctioneer told them that a "shill" bidder would participate to help bring up the bidding to the desired price. Instead, the property wound up selling for $175,000. To top the whole thing off, the courts found in the subsequent lawsuit that the auctioneer did not commit fraud and that, based on the contract, the sellers had no reason to rely on the auctioneer's statements. The family also failed to recoup any damages for the shill's failure to drive up the price, because the use of shill bidders "is contrary to public policy."

■ Because the form of the sales contract is determined prior to the auction, there are no opportunities for variations in the contract that might be more attractive overall. Only the price is determined during the auction process. Make sure that your contract covers every issue that may come up.

■ If you want to have a minimum or reserve price auction, make *certain* that the auction or sales contract says as much. If your contract says "absolute" and you want or need a reserve price, you will be stuck with an absolute auction. The courts have been ruling very clearly and consistently on this.

■ Make certain that bidder registration procedures are followed clearly. It is not unknown for auctioneers to arrange for false-flag bidders or for bidders mysteriously to "fail to complete" the bidder registration procedures because they've disappeared. One way to help deal with this is to require all bidders for your property to appear at the auction. Telephone and Internet bids that don't have valid registration procedures behind them are very easily used to manipulate the auction process.

■ Make sure that your auctioneer fully discloses all relevant information about both the property and his agency to you. Quite a few legal cases have gone through the courts over the years dealing with "failure to disclose," and it's a very common reason for buyers to refuse to complete a sales agreement, even though they have the winning bid.

13

The Last Word: Negotiating a Good Sale

You've spiffed up your house, held open houses, and now you have an offer.

What can you do to make sure that this sale makes it all the way through close of escrow?

Anyone involved in sales will tell you that negotiation is an art, not a science. Negotiation requires substantial people skills, knowledge of your own needs and wants (and the difference between them), and the ability to create situations where all parties win.

If you have any questions about your own ability to negotiate the sale of your house, let a professional do the negotiating for you. You stand to make more money that way, and you won't experience the frustration you'll feel if the deal falls through.

What Is a "Good" Sale?

A good sale is one that goes through completion and leaves both (or all) parties feeling that they've gotten the best deal they could under the circumstances. It doesn't necessarily mean that every party got everything they wanted, when they wanted it, but it does mean that the agreement is something they can live with.

The sale of a house can be fairly complicated, particularly if there are financing issues, problems with the house, or terms that require extra effort by any of the parties. But a good sale usually involves the parties' being clear what they must have up front, respecting other parties' needs, acting like adults in the negotiating process, and being willing to be flexible.

What's Important Versus What Isn't

Before any negotiating starts, it's important that you and anyone negotiating on your behalf are clear about what you must have and what you're willing to negotiate. This is the time to analyze your situation carefully and determine, for instance, if you absolutely have to have an all-cash offer or something within $5,000 of your asking price. This is also the time to consider incentives you can offer (like the pre-paid trip to Hawaii we discussed in Chapter 1) during the bargaining process to sweeten the deal.

If your house has been on the market for a long time, you're better off being more flexible about financing, for instance. If you can afford to take back a note secured by part of the equity in your house, your buyer may be better able to arrange financing for the rest of the purchase. If you can take something else of value as part of the sale—a boat or RV, for instance—you may also have a better chance of making a sale that works for all parties.

It also pays to check your existing loans and see if any can be assumed by the buyer. Your lender may not like to let a buyer take over an existing note, but if the buyer is qualified, most lenders would rather have a sale than let the loan go into default and foreclosure.

Really important is a credit check of the buyer. Most real estate agents will do this for you as part of the sale, or you can have your bank run a credit check for you. Ratings of "very good," "good," "average," etc., are based on numerical scores and vary from lender to lender. However, Fair, Isaac & Co., the company that creates the FICO score that most lenders use, basis its credit ratings on the following:

- 15 percent of the U.S. population is below 575.

- 35 percent of the U.S. population is below 675.

- 50 percent of the U.S. population is below 724.

- 70 percent of the U.S. population is below 757.

- 90 percent of the U.S. population is below 778.

While preferred buyers generally have credit ratings of 724 or better, close examination of the credit report will tell you whether a lower rating is a consistent problem or an anomaly.

One final thing to do before you get too involved in negotiations is to write up two lists:

1. The first list should include all of the terms and items that you absolutely must have as part of a sale, prioritized as to which is most important.

2. The second list should include all of the terms and items that you want to have, again prioritized as to which is most important.

These lists will be very useful later, when you're finalizing your contract.

The Negotiating Process

Receiving an offer is usually just the first step in the negotiating process. We usually consider the initial offer an invitation to a conversation, and we frequently make a counteroffer. Sometimes this process of offer-counteroffer can go back and forth a number of times, but usually this kind of "conversation" results in each side getting more of what it wants—and settling for some concessions along the way.

However, that isn't always the case. If you're using a real estate agent and so is the potential buyer, they will likely come prepared with information the feel will justify the price and terms in the offer. Your agent will present the offer to you along with advice as to whether you should accept it, make a counteroffer, or reject the offer completely. Emotions aside, what's important is for you to evaluate the offer on its merits, along with your judgment as to whether the buyer is capable of fulfilling the terms of the contract, such as making timely payments on a loan.

At each point in the offer-counteroffer process, realize that the other side has the right simply to walk away from the deal. The more insistent you are about your price and terms, the more you risk the buyer doing just that—walking away. Most people are interested in reaching a compromise, but only one that works for both sides. And because real estate agents are usually good at suggesting ways to compromise, here's where they really earn their commission.

Respecting Others' Needs

Part of the negotiation process involves recognizing what the other party needs. The skill in negotiating a contract involves knowing the difference between needs and wants. However, some of those needs can be emotional, and discerning that part can be difficult. Let's start with the easier, more objective stuff first.

The more you can find out about why the potential buyer is making an offer for your particular house at this particular time, the more likely you can negotiate a contract that meets those needs.

For instance, if the offer you receive includes a price lower than your asking price, try to find out if the buyer is simply trying to get a good deal (a want) or is expressing a need for a price she can afford. If the latter, you either must accept her price, counter with terms that make the package more to your liking, or refuse the offer. If the buyer is simply trying to find a good deal, consider countering with a slightly lower price but with some adjustments elsewhere in the contract.

At some point in the negotiating process, you're going to realize that the whole process looks a little like the game of "chicken," where each side gives a little and maybe asks for a bit more elsewhere, until one side either accepts the latest offer or rejects everything. If you find yourself in that mindset, find a way to get out of it, because selling your house is *not* a game. Remind yourself that you're trying to reach a compromise with another individual who deserves your respect and behave accordingly.

Acting Like Adults

Which brings us to another important point. Some people consider negotiating an agreement a kind of one-upmanship, where the person whose offer is accepted wins the game, leaving the other person the loser.

Countless sales personnel and consultants have made the point that successful selling isn't a win-lose game—it's a win-win game. Unless you can create a situation in your negotiations that makes both sides winners, you have probably left bad feelings somewhere along the line, and those feelings can have bad repercussions. Remember that once you've signed the contract, you usually still have time before the property changes hands, and lots of things can happen while the property is in escrow. You want the sale to conclude successfully, so don't let childish behavior ruin a good sale.

If you rant and rave during negotiations, the impression you give the other side is that you're unstable and unreliable and perhaps haven't been telling the truth about your property. If you take a low offer personally and get insulted, you're ignoring the fact that your property is available in an open market, where anyone can make you an offer. What may seem like an insultingly low price to you might actually seem like a reasonable offer to someone who's unfamiliar with the market for houses in your neighborhood.

So during the negotiating process, try to stay calm and reasonable and keep your tantrums away from public view.

Being Flexible

In a difficult market, there are usually more sellers than buyers. This means you're competing with other sellers for the attention of a limited pool of buyers, and those buyers can afford to be more demanding in their negotiations.

Even if you can't afford to lower your price, there are lots of things you can do, most of which we've already discussed elsewhere in this book, to make your property more desirable than another one nearby.

- If you can afford to be flexible about financing terms, consider the options discussed in Chapter 10.

- If you can afford to be flexible about the close of escrow, consider adjusting your closing date to something the buyer can deal with. However, remember that until the deal closes, there is always the possibility that the buyer can find a reason to back out, and you will have then had your property off the market for that time.

- If your buyer needs time to close an exchange, consider renting the property to the buyer until it can close.

- If you can afford to help the buyer with moving costs, or if you can afford to help with storing the buyer's goods for a month or two, consider that a marketing incentive on your part. It may help you close the deal.

- Don't overlook the unconventional incentives we mentioned earlier, like a week in Hawaii or a trip to Disney World in Florida. Or offer to pay for a couple of days at a local hotel while the buyer's furniture is being moved in.

Negotiating the "Want to Have" List

Remember the "must have" and "want to have" lists that you wrote earlier? During negotiations is when you want to get as many as possible of the items on your lists worked in.

That said, you should be very clear about something: be prepared to trade items on your "want to have" list to make sure that the issues on your "must have" list are addressed.

Writing a Good Contract

Most people don't realize it, but contracts don't exist for when everyone is in agreement. They really exist for when the parties to the contract disagree about something. It provides the two of you with a common reference as to the terms you agree on and how you agreed to resolve disputes over interpretation.

What this means, then, is that a good contract clearly and legally lays out all of the terms of your agreement or, as Thomas Jefferson once said, "to place before mankind the common sense of the subject, in terms so plain and firm as to command their assent."

The first thing you need to do to get your contract finalized is to sit down with whoever's helping you draft it, or your response to a contract proposed by a potential buyer, and put down all of the terms to which you and the buyer have agreed. This should just be a list of

- proposed terms, including payments and escrow closing dates; and

- any other terms needed to cover specialty items, such as transfers, exchanges, mortgage assumptions, and so forth.

Write them down, clearly. Now, make sure that everything on your "must have" list of terms is addressed. Then go back over the contract and see how much of your "want to have" list of terms has been addressed.

Next, hand that list to whoever is helping you draft the actual contract. If you're working with a real estate agent, for example, they almost certainly have access to a boilerplate contract that is used as a starting point by their brokerage. Alternately, you might go to a good real estate lawyer and have that professional draw up the contract, again probably starting from standard language.

The one thing you don't want to do, unless you're an experienced contract professional, is to write the contract yourself. Why? Because, ultimately, almost any professional will have access to a lawyer to vet the contract. And if the contract is disputed, it's going to be resolved by lawyers. So you might as well have a lawyer look at the contract *before* you sign it, rather than after it's too late and you're in a disagreement.

Once you've finally got the terms where you want them, it's time to let the buyer have a crack at the contract, if they haven't already. They're going to go through this same procedure on their end and make sure that all of their "must have" terms have been addressed as well. You may well go back and forth on the terms a bit, though you should have nailed all that down in negotiations, before writing up the actual contract.

Once you're done, go sign the contract. Don't play games with it or keep changing the terms to try to get a better deal. We've seen more deals fall apart for precisely that reason.

Index